S0-BBB-484

AMATEURS

BY DAVID AUBURN

AMATEURS was originally produced by Ensemble Studio Theatre in New York City on June 10, 2010. It was directed by Harris Yulin. The cast was as follows:

M .... David Rasche
W .... Diana Ruppe

CONTENTS

AMATEURS

A middle-aged man in a luxurious office. A young woman opposite.

W. I thought you had retired.

M. I am retired.

W. What do you do here?

M. Working on a memoir.

W. At a law firm?

M. I'm on the board. They let me have an office. It's a perk.

W. And a secretary?

M. I share an administrative assistant with one of the partners. I haven't used her much though. Frankly I got the office because I thought I'd want more of a team around me. The publisher set me up with a couple of ghosts, you know, professionals, but I met with them and we didn't really click so I thought I'd give it a crack by myself, "quill in hand" kind of thing, and you know what? I've enjoyed it. I'm not much of a writer. What am I saying? I'm not a "writer." But I've enjoyed the time to reflect, dredging up memories ... I've even enjoyed the typing, the physical production of it. Not that I know what I'm doing. The whole thing stinks, probably ... *(She looks at him. Beat.)* Would you like something to drink?

W. Sure, a glass of water would be ... *(He picks up the phone.)*

M. Penny? Could we have a water? Oh — *(To W.)* Ice?

W. Sure.

M. Ice. And *(Laughs.)* no, uh-uh, hey, it's not eleven o'clock. Don't you dare! Penny ... Agh. This is not fair, you're killing me. *(He hangs up.)* Three Cokes before noon, *maximum,* I try to space them out. She tries to tempt me ... it's ... anyway. Have a seat.

W. Thank you. *(She sits.)*

M. So.

W. So. Is my dad in your memoir?

M. Who's your dad?

W. She didn't tell you? Penny?

M. She said someone was coming to ask me some questions about my work.

W. Nothing else?

M. I'm always happy to talk about my work. My old work. We don't screen people out. Who is your father?

W. Thomas Martin.

M. No kidding!

W. Yes.

M. Tom Martin! Sure, I remember the daughters. Jackie and Eve, right?

W. Right.

M. Which one are you?

W. Eve.

M. You're younger, right?

W. Right.

M. How's Jackie?

W. She's fine.

M. What does she do? My God, I remember you two as angelic little things, you were probably about what, about seven? And Jackie was twelve?

W. You have a good memory.

M. I used to have a very good memory. Some things stick, some don't. It helps to write about it, it's surprising how much comes back. You were both lovely.

W. Thank you.

M. You were assets. Tom was smart to have you around so much. You still look wonderful.

W. Thank you. *(Penny enters with the drinks.)*

PENNY. Here you go.

W. Thanks.

PENNY. And for you …

M. Oh God, she did it …

PENNY. Yessir.

M. Uh-oh, I'm screwed. Gotta drink it now, it's here … *(Penny chuckles as she exits.)*

M. What does Jackie do?

W. She's an attorney in Florida.

M. Good for her.

W. Civil rights stuff. Employment discrimination …

M. Uh-huh, good! And you?

W. I was a runner.

M. A runner? You mean like a jogger?

W. Track.

M. Professional?

W. Yes.

M. Well, that's something. Wow. An athlete. Good for you. You must be very good.

W. Not first rank, but good.

M. Olympics?

W. Sydney.

M. No kidding.

W. Four hundred. Came in eighth in a field of eleven.

M. I'd call that first rank. I mean, Olympics, my goodness. "Eighth" means eighth-best in the *world*.

W. I wasn't really trained to think that way. Medals are all that counts.

M. That's bullshit. You were in the Olympics. How many people can say that?

W. Thousands.

M. And now?

W. Mom.

M. How many?

W. One. Boy.

M. Good for you. I have a girl. Caroline.

W. Yes?

M. Yep. She's uh — well, I suppose she's a little younger than you.

W. And what does she do?

M. She's actually still discovering what it is that she really … she's a *terrific* kid, very smart, *very* intense, but she hasn't quite found her … she's not exactly Olympic material, is the thing.

W. Oh.

M. *Yet.*

W. Yes.

M. But she's amazing. She … Anyway. *(Beat.)* I've always wondered about that Olympic Village.

W. What about it?

M. What's it like?

W. A big dorm.

M. It must be pretty wild.

W. What do you mean?

M. I mean, all those young athletes cooped up together, all those finely tuned bodies, the most perfect bodies in the *world* ... all that adrenaline ... It must be just a two-week boink-fest. *(Beat.)*

W. This isn't really what I came to talk about.

M. No, no, of course not. What can I do for you?

W. Well, my dad had a stroke ...

M. Oh, God, I'm so sorry to hear that.

W. Thank you.

M. How is he?

W. Not very well.

M. Oh no.

W. Paralyzed on one side, and his speech is pretty heavily impaired.

M. That is just awful. I am so sorry. He was such a wonderful speaker.

W. Yes, it's pretty bad. He's still all there mentally ...

M. Thank God for that.

W. Yes.

M. That's the important thing. It may not seem like it now, but that's huge, actually. The other things can change, given time.

W. That's what they keep telling us.

M. Believe it. It's amazing what the human body is capable of. Especially when — your dad was an athlete himself, wasn't he? Baseball, right? Wasn't he All-American in college?

W. That's right. Good memory.

M. Well, he had the coaching the Little League thing in his ads, that was tremendous. That was an asset. We had *no* idea what to do with that one. You can't mess around with something like that, it's just iconic. He nearly turned pro, didn't he?

W. He played minor league ball for a while. It's how he worked his way through law school.

M. Oh, yeah, that was beautiful, too. Third baseman by day, hitting the books all night, working his way up from ... Your grandfather was, what, some sort of clerk?

W. Owned a drugstore.

M. Right, the drugstore, soda fountain ... Baseball, the two beautiful little girls ... great. How's your mom handling it?

W. She died a couple years ago.

M. Oh dear. Eve, I'm sorry. I keep saying that ...

W. Listen, I'm not here to break your heart. My sister and I are setting up a little foundation in honor of my dad. It's something he's talked about for a long time. If he — when he gets better he'll run it. It's — we've done a formal statement of purpose, I can give you a copy of the draft prospectus, but basically we're just gonna try to work on the issues Dad cared about. Cares about.

M. And you're looking for donors.

W. Yes.

M. I'd be honored. I would. However I can help out. *(She looks at him for a moment longer than is comfortable.)*

W. Thank you.

M. What are your plans?

W. We're still working out the specifics. But as you know, Dad was very, very interested in social justice.

M. Uh-huh.

W. He was passionate about civil rights, as you know, and education. So we're looking at funding a number of programs, pilot programs that would further those goals.

M. Which goals?

W. Greater social justice and, and equity ... and access to education — scholarships is one thing we're looking at.

M. Good.

W. Environmental awareness, fostering that ... And we have some other ideas. Activist training. And there'll be a website —

M. Good, web presence very important.

W. More than a site, an online *community*, would ultimately be part of the — and you know, hopefully we'll just be a presence and a force — well, *force* is too strong. A —

M. Player?

W. A driving — well, yes, a force in the broader community, the progressive community ...

M. Great.

W. I know that's not exactly your, uh —

M. No, listen: Big picture, we're all on the same side, right? A strong civic life, preserving, contributing to the enrichment of the national conversation —

W. Exactly. That's the kind of thing we — It's all in the prospectus, but —

M. No, it sounds terrific. Where do I sign?

W. *(Laughs.)* Well, we —

M. Have you got the board in place?

W. Well the board is still in formation.

M. What's your give or get?

W. Um. I …

M. Do you know what that means? *(She doesn't.)* When you form a board of directors, you establish a minimum annual figure that each member must either contribute themselves or raise from contributions from others. Right? That way you end up with an effective table, and not just, you know, your sister's best friend from college —

W. Right. Right.

M. Make sense?

W. Yes. Of course. Thanks. *(Beat.)* So, should I just leave you the prospectus, or —

M. I'll write you a check now. *(He takes out his checkbook.)*

W. You don't have to do that now.

M. Don't be silly, you're not walking away empty-handed. Have you got an amount in mind? Have you set some sort of Founder's Level or something?

W. No. We hadn't really talked about that.

M. You're not just going around asking people for whatever amount, I hope.

W. I guess we are.

M. How much are you hoping to raise? Altogether.

W. Long-term? Or —

M. What's your fantasy?

W. I guess, if we ended up with an endowment of, I don't know, two million, we think we could —

M. Is that in the prospectus?

W. No. It's just something Jackie and I've talked about.

M. Aim for five. Put it in the prospectus. Say you want to raise that in the first year —

W. *(Laughs.)* The first year?

M. You have to inspire people. Don't aim low and don't be coy, be very clear about what you want and what you expect. Establish a floor for the first round of giving, all the people you're approaching now, call it the "Founders Circle" or the "Pioneers Fund" … $10,000 to be a Founder.

W. I can't ask people for $10,000.

M. Of course you can. You just asked me.

W. To *listen*, that's all —

M. What did you think I'd give?

W. I don't know.

M. What did you *hope* I'd give?

W. Five hundred dollars?

M. *(Laughs.)* You insult me. *(He hands her a check. She looks at it.)*

W. Wow. *(Beat. She keeps looking at the check.)* Why did you run that ad?

M. Which ad is that?

W. You know, the one of my dad kissing a man.

M. Because your dad kissed a man. *(Beat.)*

W. Will that be in the memoir?

M. I haven't gotten to the eighties yet. *(Beat.)*

W. At a victory celebration. *Years* earlier. It was a huge upset, his first win. Everyone was drunk with disbelief, *everyone* was kissing him, hugging him. One of my dad's oldest friends embraced him. My mom was standing right there. She was holding a baby, my sister. You cropped them out of the photo ...

M. Listen, if you want to talk about this I'm happy to talk about it, but it wasn't necessary to go through all the "foundation" bullshit.

W. It's not bullshit.

M. You and your sister really are starting this thing?

W. Of course.

M. And you want *my* money?

W. I wanted to see what you'd say.

M. All right.

W. I wanted to see if you'd be hypocritical enough to ... You're *sickening*. You ... *(Takes a breath.)* You practice a brand of politics ... your whole approach is so alien, so antithetical to our, to this country's aspirations ... it's because of people like you that the whole *process* is poisoned. The whole poisoned process is ... you are *contemptible*. And you need to hear that. You should be *ashamed. (Beat.)*

M. That what you came to say?

W. Yes.

M. Okay then.

W. Okay.

M. You gonna keep the check?

W. I wanted to know what you'd do if I —

M. You gonna keep it?

W. Yes.

M. You definitely should. You'd be crazy not to.

W. I am.

M. Okay, then. Take care. *(He picks up the phone.)* Penny? Okay, I'm free, could you —

W. How can you *live* with yours —

M. *(Sighs.)* Hang on.

W. Is there *anything* you wouldn't do?

M. I wouldn't kiss a black man on the mouth in public and be photographed doing it if I were running for political office. We could start there. I mean, that seems pretty basic.

W. You dig up this old photo. You crop out my mother. You crop out his baby, the forty other people on the stage ... you play to the *ugliest* — it was *eleven years earlier* —

M. The picture was published. It was in the record. I should have ignored it? By the way, and I don't know if this will make you feel any better — it probably won't — but I think we would have won even if we hadn't used it.

W. Then why did you use it?

M. Because we had it. Because he did it. So no I don't lose sleep over it. If we hadn't used it, and lost, I would have lost sleep over *that*, but — *(Beat. She rips his check in half.)*

M. Attagirl. That'll teach me.

W. Fuck you.

M. Lovely. *(On phone.)* Penny? Sorry. We're done, thanks. Would you —

W. I'm not done.

M. Eve Martin, you are rude. You come to *my* office. I don't want to have to call downstairs. *(They look at each other. Beat.)*

W. Before I go, will you read that?

M. I'm sorry? *(She indicates the envelope.)* If you think I'm writing you another check ...

W. I think you should at least look at it.

M. Your "*foundation*"? What is the point? *(She crosses her arms, stares at him.)*

M. *(Sighs.)* Oh my heavens. You're just wasting your time with this thing. I have to believe on some level you must understand that. I mean, if you had taken my check and gone out and spent it on shoes or a trip to Florence, I wouldn't have minded at all, I'd actually have been happy that my money wasn't going to waste, because it would have gone to waste at your foundation, assuming you ever get it off the ground, which I seriously doubt, since you don't know a tax deduction from your sister's asshole. *(She doesn't move.)* Whatever money you raise, you're just going to squander it on a lot of, what, "activist training" or some garbage, so a lot of other nice, polite, expensively educated girls and boys can learn to very politely "organize" for nice candidates who like to hear themselves talk about "social justice" and "fairness" and "speaking truth to power," whatever the fuck *that* means (I've never figured it out), and accomplish *nothing,* and then get depressed and start thinking about starting some sort of socially "responsible" business like marketing your own line of fair-trade shampoo or shade-grown, what, *granola … (She doesn't move.)* Seriously, listen to me, and I say this out of the goodness of my heart: There is no purpose — *no purpose, none* — in anything you've done or anything you are dreaming of doing. Okay, Eve? And that is what you people do not understand. Agh, you're so *smug.* Look at you. You're so *pure.* Not like me. I'm a *racist.* Right? Oooooh. I'm *homophobic!* All that grad-school — I'm "speaking in code" to my "racist, homophobic base." Right? No. Wrong. No. I put a photo of your dad like that in an ad, like I did, the message I am sending, EVE, is not "My opponent is a nigger-loving faggot." Okay? The message is: *My opponent is naïve and careless and weak for letting a photo like this be taken, the silly fuck.* That is the message. That is the message that I send and that is received. And none of you get that, and that is why you lose and go on losing. *(Picks up his phone.)* Penny. I am *very sorry.* I — *(Eve doesn't move. She just looks at him. He shakes his head, puts down the phone, takes the papers out of the envelope, gives them a cursory glance. Then reads more.)* What is this? You have got to be kidding me. Who — *(He flips to the end.)* Jacqueline Martin? What is this?

W. It's an affidavit.

M. I — This is not a —

W. My sister wanted you to have a copy.

M. Oh, you have got to be kidding me. This is a joke, right?

W. A copy goes to the head of this firm. And every member of the board. And to your wife.

M. And to what does this "affidavit" attest, exactly?

W. That backstage at the first debate of Tom Martin's last campaign you touched his older daughter inappropriately, and made obscene comments to her. She was twelve.

M. That is absurd.

W. Well. *(Beat.)*

15

M. This is not even a — this is just a piece of paper.

W. It's legal. She's a lawyer.

M. Oh, come on. *(He reads.)* You two are ridiculous. This is — is that what you want? Some sort of he-said/she-said thing? No one will believe it. And they shouldn't, because it isn't true.

W. And we're going to go to the press.

M. And say what?

W. That on an October night fifteen years ago, when you were running the campaign against Tom Martin, you tried to get his 12-year-old daughter to perform a sexual act. That first you asked her to, and then when she wouldn't, you threatened. It's all in the affidavit. That's your copy.

M. You sent it to my wife?

W. We will. And everyone you work with. And the publisher of your memoir will know about this, too.

M. Unless what?

W. You don't understand. I don't think you should have this office. And I don't think you should be getting a three-million-dollar advance from your publisher for publishing your memoir. And I don't think you should have a happy marriage, not after what you did to my family. I don't think your kids should look up to you. And I don't think you should have this reputation you have, this sort of "lovable rogue," or "What a *rascal,* he certainly pushed the envelope, he bent the rules a little but, wow he knew how to play the game, you've got to give him that," that whole thing. You know? I don't think you should get invited to dinner parties. I don't think you should be on boards of directors, I don't think talk shows should call you up and put you on and treat you like you're some kind of wise elder statesman, someone respectable, instead of a lying piece of filth who pollutes every-thing, which is what you are. I don't think you should be able to show your face in public. I don't think you should have any of it. Neither does Jackie. We may not be able to take it *all* away from you. But we'll — *(His telephone buzzes.)* We'll *try* —

M. Excuse me. *(On phone.)* Yes. Right, I know, thank you, Penny. Sorry about before. I — One minute. *(To W.)* I have another meeting.

W. Fine. You think about that. *(She starts to go.)*

M. Wait a minute. Eve. *(She stops.)* Does your father know you're doing this?

W. Of course not.

M. I didn't think so.

W. What does that mean?

M. The Tom Martin I know would be ashamed if he knew his daughter was involved in something like this.

W. The Tom Martin you know?

M. One of the most decent men I've ever met in politics. One of the most decent men *period.* And his daughters turn out like this ...

W. You don't know him.

M. This is just sad. Do you think your dad, if he knew — you say he's still all there mentally, if that's true — if he could comprehend that you're here now peddling some filth about his little girl Jackie giving blow jobs —

W. We're not saying she did it. We're saying you *asked* her to, because you *did* —

M. I can't imagine what ... I think he'd cry. I think tears would roll down his paralyzed face. I saw your dad cry at the dedication of the Vietnam Memorial, 1982, touching the name of the best friend who never came home with him, that picture they took of *that* sent his numbers through the roof, because it was *honest,* like him, uncalculating, authentic, *decent. Everybody* who knew your father thought of him as the most decent man they'd ever met, an e*xample.*

W. And you destroyed him.

M. Not because I didn't like him! I liked him just like everybody else! And I know he was so proud of you and Jackie, and I cannot *imagine* what he'd say if he knew you were standing in my office right now trying to do what you are trying to do. He — *(Beat.)* Does your *sister* even know you're doing this?

W. Jackie and I —

M. Oh my goodness. She doesn't. I bet she doesn't.

W. Jackie —

M. I bet if I called her up right now and said, Jackie, your crazy little sister Eve, who crapped out in Sydney and never recovered, is blackmailing me with some sleazy sex story involving you when you were *twelve* —

W. You don't know anything about *her,* or *me,* or my *family* —

M. And what about your mother? Have you thought about her? My goodness. Your poor mother, God rest her soul. *(She looks at him.)*

W. That's good. You are good. But it won't help you now. *(Takes a breath.)* "The arc of history is long —"

M. No, please don't use that quote.

W. "— but it curves toward justice." Martin Luther King. Think about that.

M. Okay, look. Wait. Eve. Come on. Let's — Listen to me. Just — I want you to hear me out, okay? It's only fair.

W. *(Laughs.)* Fair?

M. It's only — look, you're going to throw the Reverend at me, you're going to fling this dirt, the least you can do is listen, all right? Your dad would. He was a great listener. *(She folds her arms.)* I am not saying, I have never said that everything I've done in my life has succeeded in — has been in the furtherance of complete, whatever, *comity,* or — I am not saying I have no regrets, and I am not unaware that I have done things in my work and in my life that have caused pain. I know that. I am *deeply* aware of that, believe me. But I have also done things that have *saved* people pain. I have *prevented* anguish. I have gone out of my way on a *number* of occasions — I can't go into details but that is absolutely the case, you have to believe me. And I understand the feelings of a daughter for her father. I do. I understand the pain you experience on his behalf. That's a credit to you. I have a kid, for heaven's sake. I have my own little girl. I know that she is the source of all the joy and all the anguish in *my* world, I have to imagine at least *some* of that is reciprocated. And, no denying, we have had our problems in the past and I, as I sit here listening to you and watching what you're doing, appalling and sleazy and dishonest as it is, part of me envies the bond that the risk you're taking represents. I mean, nuts as you are, you clearly love your dad and would do anything for him. And I wish — okay, yes: I wish I could be certain … that I knew that my daughter felt the degree of … the same way about me, and I … *(Beat.)* Do you know what this would do to *her?* Even the accusation. Even to hear it, what that would do to what is already a fragile … Have you thought how this would make Caroline feel? I'm not talking about my wife. Or the partners at this firm, I'm talking about my *daughter. (Beat. She looks at him.)*

W. I'm sorry. *(She turns to go.)*

M. Eve. I'm asking you. Please. *(Beat.)*

W. No. *(Beat.)*

M. Okay. I understand. Then before you leave there's just one more thing I have to do. *(He sighs, heavy. Picks up the phone.)* Penny? Hi. No, I am going need another *(Looks at his watch.)* two minutes here, yes. And — oh, no, I don't need another Coke, that's — yeah, just listen for a sec, okay? Right now could you bring me a file box, it's in with the research materials, labeled 84. I think it's got a green lid. It should be right out — Perfect. Thanks. *(He hangs up.)* Luckily, I've got all my files here. The memoir. They gave me an extra room next door. It's a good set-up. Saves a lot of time. *(Awkward beat as they wait. Penny enters. She puts a file box on his desk.)*

PENNY. Here you go.

M. Great. Thanks a million. *(As Penny exits.)* Two minutes.

W. What are you —

M. Here we go. *(M. pulls out a very thick file. Then another.)* Stuff from the '84 campaign. Tom Martin. Oh, there's another one. *(He pulls out a third file.)* Oppo research. This takes me back. *(Sighs.)* Okay, so … *(He opens a file at random and pulls out a document.)* Encounter with Tom Martin in a bus station restroom in New Haven, 1961. He was young, we all make mistakes. This affidavit *is* legal, by the way. *(He searches some more.)* Right. Tom Martin spotted — oh, and photographed — by numerous witnesses in a variety of gay bars and clubs in New York City, San Francisco, Los Angeles, Boston, Chicago, Atlanta, Detroit, Memphis, Miami, New Orleans, Denver, Philadelphia, Cincinnati throughout the 1970s … Cincinnati? Tom Martin arrested for lewd behavior in a park in Boston, 1977. Hm. You were what, about three? He covered that up with help from some friends. We found it though. Should I go on? He kept a special apartment in New York City from 1967 to 1974 … This is a list of men who were willing to go on record with sex with your dad. We have one *videotape,* my goodness. I don't want to … Eve, I'm sorry, but we had evidence of your dad on his knees with a cock in his mouth pretty much continuously from the early Sixties on. We never had to use it. That one photo was enough. You should be *grateful. (Beat. W. stares in shock.)*

W. I …

M. Okay? *(He packs up the box.)* See, this is why you come in *eighth.* I mean, running in the *Olympics* in front of a *billion* people and you come in eighth? How does that feel? Not even, like, third? *Eighth?* How do you recover from *that?* You don't, I guess. See, that is what I always hated about your dad and all you people. You're amateurs. You know, you show up for a *game* — *(He picks up her "affidavit" and tosses it at her contemptuously. He picks up the phone.)* Penny? Thanks. We're done.

End of Play

PROPERTY LIST

Phone
Drinks: water, Coke
Checkbook
Pen
Affadavit
File box
Thick file
Documents

SOUND EFFECTS

Phone buzzer

BOLERO

BY DAVID IVES

BOLERO

Middle of the night. Complete darkness, growing to a low area light on a bed. Behind the bed, a wall. A Woman and a Man, asleep under a sheet. Very, very faintly — the sound of a wind. Then it's gone. A moment passes. The Woman sits up suddenly in bed.

WOMAN. *(Gasps in fright.)* Huh…! *(She sits listening, looking into the darkness around the bed.)*

MAN. *(Head on pillow, rubs her shoulder.)* Shhhh … *(She lies back down and pulls the sheet up over herself. She settles herself. A moment. Then, very faintly again — the sound of a rushing wind. The woman sits up again.)*

WOMAN. What was that? *(She listens.)* Did you hear something?

MAN. *(Head still on pillow.)* Huh?

WOMAN. I heard something. *(She looks into the darkness around the bed, listening. Nothing.)*

MAN. *(Puts a hand on her shoulder and rubs it.)* Shhhh … It's the wind. *(Slowly, she lies back down and pulls the sheet up over herself. She settles herself. A moment. Then, faintly — the sound of a rushing wind. The woman sits up again.)*

WOMAN. What was that?

MAN. Huh? What … ?

WOMAN. Didn't you hear something?

MAN. What's the matter? *(She listens.)*

WOMAN. I think somebody's in the apartment. *(She looks into the darkness around the bed, listening. The shadows around the bed roil, slightly.)*

MAN. It's just the wind. Go back to sleep. Shhhh … *(Slowly, as before, she lies back down and starts to pull up the sheet, but sits up again.)*

WOMAN. There. Listen.

MAN. What time is it…?

WOMAN. Listen.

MAN. *(Raises his head from the pillow a little.)* I don't hear anything. *(Lowers his head back to the pillow.)* Go back to sleep. *(Puts a hand up and rubs her shoulder.)* Go back to sleep. Shhhh … *(She lies back down and pulls the blanket up over herself as before. She settles herself. A moment. Then, the sound of a rushing wind. The Woman sits up and turns on a lamp.)*

WOMAN. Wake up. *(Nothing.)* Wake up. *(Listens.)* There's somebody in the apartment.

MAN. Huh?

WOMAN. Somebody's in the apartment.

MAN. What…? Somebody what…?

WOMAN. Didn't you hear that? *(The Man lifts his head and listens a moment.)* Listen.

MAN. I don't hear anything.

WOMAN. You didn't hear that?

MAN. *(Lowering his head back down.)* What time is it…?

WOMAN. Right there. You didn't hear it?

MAN. What did you hear?

WOMAN. I heard a noise. Listen.

MAN. You're dreaming. *(The sound of a wind, for a moment.)*

WOMAN. You didn't hear that?

MAN. It's just the wind under the door. *(They listen a moment more.)*

WOMAN. No, I heard a noise.

MAN. *(Rubbing her shoulder.)* Shhhh. Go back to sleep.

WOMAN. *(Calls.)* Hello!

MAN. SHHH!

WOMAN. HELLO! *(She listens.)*

MAN. See? There's nobody. It's nothing. *(He turns off the lamp. She keeps listening.)* Come on. Come here. *(He puts a hand on her back.)* Come down here. *(She slides down beside him.)* Slide in close.

WOMAN. No.

MAN. Come on. Slide in very close. *(He pulls the sheet up over them.)*

WOMAN. No.

MAN. I want you to slide in very tight.

WOMAN. I heard something.

MAN. You think you heard something.

WOMAN. I know I heard something.

MAN. Shhh …

WOMAN. God, I hate the night. *(Suddenly, louder and quite distinct — the sound of a rushing wind. She sits up.)* What was that?

24

MAN. What?

WOMAN. You didn't hear that? *(She sits up on the side of the bed and turns on the lamp.)*

MAN. I didn't hear anything.

WOMAN. How could you not hear that? It was a person.

MAN. What time is it?

WOMAN. I think it was from next door. *(Indicating the wall behind the bed.)* From there.

MAN. You think you heard something —

WOMAN. I know I did.

MAN. What did it sound like?

WOMAN. Shhh! *(She listens.)*

MAN. What did it sound like?

WOMAN. It sounded like a groan. A person groaning.

MAN. You have been known to have a dangerous imagination …

WOMAN. Shhh! *(She listens.)*

MAN. Maybe somebody's making love.

WOMAN. No. It wasn't like that.

MAN. This isn't the first time you thought you —

WOMAN. Shhh! I did hear it this time. *(She listens.)* Who lives over there? Is it that guy?

MAN. What guy?

WOMAN. The tall guy, the dark guy, in the elevator.

MAN. The tall dark guy in the elevator. This is your imagination.

WOMAN. You've seen him. You said so.

MAN. Oh, that tall dark guy. *(She listens near the wall.)* Can we go back to sleep now? What time is it? *(She keeps listening.)* Would you like a stethoscope, to hear better? Or a glass? Put it against the wall …

WOMAN. It was a person.

MAN. All right.

WOMAN. I think it was a woman.

MAN. Do you hear the person now?

WOMAN. No. I did hear somebody.

MAN. Come back to bed. Come on.

WOMAN. Listen. *(Very faintly — men's voices. We can't make out the words.)* Voices.

MAN. Okay. *(The listen a moment.)* Doesn't sound like a woman. Doesn't sound like anything.

WOMAN. Two men.

25

MAN. Two men. Talking in the middle of the night. That's very sinister, two men talking in the middle of the night.

WOMAN. Have we ever heard voices from over there before?

MAN. We've never listened before.

WOMAN. They must be talking very loudly.

MAN. They're probably listening to us and laughing.

WOMAN. I don't recognize the voices.

MAN. They're sitting up in bed, saying, "Listen. Somebody's on the other side of that wall! They've got a glass to the wall right now."

WOMAN. What's on the other side of this wall?

MAN. Oh God …

WOMAN. Is it a bedroom? Is it a kitchen? SHHH!

MAN. Well, I'm very awake now. What time is it? *(A woman's voice floats up, faintly. We can't make out any of her words.)*

WOMAN. There is a woman.

MAN. All right. Now we know what's on the other side of the wall. Two men and a woman.

WOMAN. Why can we hear them tonight? And who are those people?

MAN. Shhh.

WOMAN. What's happening on the other side of this wall

MAN. Shhh …

WOMAN. *(Starting to get agitated.)* Who are those people?

MAN. Shhhhhhhhhhh.

WOMAN. Who are those people? What's happening on the other side of the wall? What's happening … *(She is getting very agitated.)*

MAN. Breathe. Breathe. That's right.

WOMAN. I'm so afraid.

MAN. Shhh. I know.

WOMAN. I'm so afraid all the time.

MAN. In deep, hold it. Out again. In deep, hold it in. Out again.

WOMAN. It's when night starts to fall.

MAN. I know.

WOMAN. Sometimes I think the building is going to collapse on top of me. Just from the weight of it up there, all that concrete and steel. The whole thing will crumble.

MAN. Keep breathing.

WOMAN. Chicken Little. The sky is falling.

MAN. Breathe.

WOMAN. But what about when you have a right to be afraid? What about when you ought to be afraid?

MAN. There's nothing to be afraid about. Shhh ...

WOMAN. What's happening on the other side of that wall?

MAN. You looked so cool the first time I ever saw you. So secure. So serene.

WOMAN. Sometimes I think I'd love to spend my life walking from house to house, knocking on people's doors and asking if I can come in, to see how they live.

MAN. You looked so strong.

WOMAN. To see what their places are like on the inside, behind the windows. All across the country.

MAN. It all seemed to come from some deep well of happiness and goodness.

WOMAN. Having a cup of coffee today, looking through the windows of the coffee shop, watching all the people pass by, I thought, what lives are all those people having? Then I saw two men standing on the corner talking about something, and it took me a second, but it was you.

MAN. Shhh ...

WOMAN. I hadn't recognized you.

MAN. Shhh ...

WOMAN. How could I not recognize you? *(A sudden very loud, dull thump is heard. The Woman gets out of bed.)*

MAN. Whoa! *(Silence.)* What was that?

WOMAN. What was that? You heard that.

MAN. What was it? *(They listen.)*

WOMAN. Something fell. *(Voices from the other side for a moment, excited. Then the voices fade.)* We have to do something.

MAN. Do something?

WOMAN. Yes. We have to.

MAN. What can we do? About what?

WOMAN. You heard that, too.

MAN. What did we hear?

WOMAN. You heard it.

MAN. But what was it? Somebody dropped a mustard jar, making a midnight snack.

WOMAN. It didn't sound like a mustard jar.

MAN. What did it sound like? What do you think it was? A body?

WOMAN. Shhh! *(They listen.)* It's quiet now. No voices.

MAN. They went to bed. They've eaten their sandwiches and now they're going to sleep. After stuffing the woman's body down the garbage disposal.

WOMAN. I'm not just dreaming. I'm not imagining something. You heard it, too.

MAN. But we don't know what we heard.

WOMAN. Terrible things do happen. Shit happens. Bodies down garbage disposals. STOP LAUGHING AT ME.

MAN. I'm not laughing at you.

WOMAN. Who says something terrible isn't happening right over there, on the other side of this wall?

MAN. Who says it's not some people having a little party on the other side of this wall. Do you hear anything? Any horrible sounds? Any screams? So is there anything to worry about?

WOMAN. God, I hate it.

MAN. The wind under the door.

WOMAN. God, I hate the nighttime.

MAN. Shhh. *(He puts a hand on her shoulder and rubs it.)* Come on back to bed. Come on. *(She gets into bed and he pulls the cover up over her.)* Slide in close.

WOMAN. No.

MAN. I want you to slide in nice and tight.

WOMAN. No … *(Moment.)*

MAN. God, I used to love the night, the middle of the night. Three o'clock in the morning. Staying up all night till dawn. Remember that? That time of night before dawn when it isn't night anymore, it isn't any time, time stops and you feel like you're going to live forever and the world's always going to be as still and pale, pale blue as this. And the joy, when you feel that light approach. Filling the street. Then it is dawn and there are people in the street and you go out for breakfast, feeling a little bit like hell, but elated. Elated. Like you know something all those other people don't know who didn't stay up. That knowledge you get by staying up all night and seeing the dawn. *(We hear the muffled cry of a woman.)*

WOMAN. What was that? What was that? *(Again, the muffled cry of a woman, more intense.)* What was that? *(The cry comes again. Then the sound of a woman, gasping. They listen.)*

MAN. I told you. Somebody's making love.

WOMAN. They're not making love.

MAN. Are you kidding? They're fucking their brains ov
cries go on. Woman gets out of bed and stands at the wall.)
WOMAN. They're not fucking. That woman is in pain.
MAN. Just listen. It's two people fucking. *(The cries go on, more*
dimly.) Definitely fucking. *(The cries stop.)* And now they've
stopped. They're satisfied. They've gotten the pleasure that's due to
them. They're going to sleep. They're slipping off to dreamland.
WOMAN. Sometimes in the middle of the night I think, what if
those people are right about God. That there is a God who watch-
es us all the time, every moment, every one of us.
MAN. An old man with a white beard.
WOMAN. No.
MAN. Babies with harps and wings?
WOMAN. A God who punishes. Who's keeping track of every
move we make, and if you do the wrong thing, you burn. Period.
No questions. No clemency. You sin — you suffer. For all eternity.
Because it doesn't matter what you want God to be. It's not like
after you die you can say, I'm sorry, you are not the God I believe
in. My God is not a torturer, I believe in a loving God, I believe in
a kinder gentler God. It's too late by then. You've been found wanting, you've been weighed in the scale, you fucked up, you blew
your chance and now you're going to suffer for it forever. And
there's nobody you can appeal to, you don't get to go to some other
God and say, you're the God I want, help me. But how do you
know what's the right thing? Or the wrong thing? To this torturer
God? And when you've done them? How do you know when
you've condemned yourself, when you've crossed the line, how do
you know how to escape eternal punishment?
MAN. Come back to bed.
WOMAN. No.
MAN. Come on, slide in close.
WOMAN. No …
MAN. I want you to slide in nice and tight.
WOMAN. No!
MAN. Come on. Come on.
WOMAN. Goddamn it, I said *NO! (Suddenly, we hear a woman*
cry out, loud and close.)
MAN. Jesus…!
VOICE OF WOMAN. Help me. Help me…! Oh, God, help me …
WOMAN. Did you hear that?

MAN. She called out.

WOMAN. She said *help me*. She said help me, what are we going to do?

MAN. Wait a minute.

WOMAN. What are we going to do?

MAN. Just stay calm. Stay calm ...

WOMAN. *(Over second "stay calm.")* You heard it, too.

MAN. We don't know what's going on over there.

WOMAN. Did you not hear her?

MAN. I don't hear anything now. It's quiet.

WOMAN. She said *help me*.

MAN. Maybe she didn't. Anyway it's quiet now. It's over, whatever it was.

WOMAN. No, it's not. *(Muffled, the sound of a woman crying.)* She's crying.

MAN. Maybe not.

WOMAN. What if that's her place, what if somebody got into her apartment?

MAN. You don't know what you're talking about ...

WOMAN. What if somebody's hurting her?

MAN. Maybe she's having a lovers' quarrel.

WOMAN. A lovers' quarrel.

MAN. Yes. Who knows?

WOMAN. Saying *help me*?

MAN. We don't know who's over there. Maybe she says thing like that while she's fucking. Maybe she screams, *Oh, God, help me.* We don't know.

WOMAN. SHHH! *(She listens.)*

MAN. We have no idea what's going on over there —

WOMAN. SHHH! Listen. *(She listens..)* Oh my God. *(Muffled voices..)* Oh my God. *(The voices get louder.)* They're beating her. Somebody's beating her.

MAN. You're imagining things.

WOMAN. *(Over him.)* I'm not imagining things. That woman is being hit.

MAN. This is a panic attack, this is an episode ... *(Together.)*

WOMAN. No, no, no, no, no, no, no, no ...

MAN. Will you just listen? LISTEN! There's nothing. Nothing. Are you hearing anything but the inside of your head? Do you ever hear anything but the inside of your own head?

WOMAN. I do hear something and I'm calling the police.

MAN. No, you're not.

WOMAN. *(Grabbing phone.)* Oh, yes, I am.

MAN. *(Trying to take the phone from her.)* You have ruined my life with this neurotic bullshit.

WOMAN. They're beating her up, for Christ's sake!

MAN. Put the phone down.

WOMAN. I'm calling the police.

MAN. I said PUT IT DOWN! *(He grabs the phone from her.)*

WOMAN. Then I'm going over there. *(She starts pulling on a robe.)*

MAN. No.

WOMAN. I'm going over there and I'm knocking on their door.

MAN. No ...

WOMAN. What do you mean, no.

MAN. You can't just hammer on somebody's door in the middle of the night.

WOMAN. I can.

MAN. You don't know what's going on.

WOMAN. They're beating   MAN. Will you listen to me,
her up, for Christ's sake.   will you listen?

WOMAN. What's on the other side of that wall? Who are those people?

MAN. Listen to me.

WOMAN. Who are you?

MAN. Listen to me.

WOMAN. I know who you are.

MAN. You're having an attack, a panic attack.

WOMAN. You can't put this off on me. You're a coward. You're a goddamn fucking coward.

MAN. Wait a minute —

WOMAN. That woman is   MAN. Okay. Okay. Okay.
getting hurt. They could kill her.

MAN. Okay! I'll go over there! I'll knock on their door and see what's going on! All right?

WOMAN. *(To the wall.)* STOP THAT! STOP IT! STOP IT! WE CAN HEAR YOU! WE'RE CALLING THE POLICE! NOW STOP IT! *(Sudden silence. Moments pass.)*

MAN. It's quiet again.

WOMAN. It's quiet again.

MAN. Right? Do you hear anything?

31

WOMAN. Oh God oh God oh God. We have fucked up. We have done the wrong thing …

MAN. It stopped now. You stopped it.

WOMAN. We have done things we ought not to have done and we have not done things we ought to have done.

MAN. Do you hear anything?

WOMAN. She could be dead.

MAN. No. Listen …

WOMAN. She's dead.

MAN. She's not dead. It *stopped*.

WOMAN. They beat her up and we didn't stop them, she called out for help and we didn't do anything, they killed her and we let them do it, we killed her too, she was calling out for help from us and we killed her.	MAN. Will you stop it? Will you stop it? We didn't do anything wrong. We didn't do anything. We didn't know what was going on over there. Now will you stop it? Will you stop it?

MAN. I said STOP IT! *(Shaking her, hard.)* STOP IT! *(He raises his hand. Loud knocking is heard. The Man and Woman are still.)*

POLICEMAN'S VOICE. *(Offstage.)* Open up in there! It's the police! *(The stage is flooded with a hard bright white light in which the Man and Woman stand frozen. We hear a deafening crash, as of a building collapsing. Blackout.)*

End of Play

PROPERTY LIST

Lamp
Phone

SOUND EFFECTS

Wind
Men's voices, faint
Woman's voice
Loud, dull thump
Excited voices
Woman's muffled cry, louder, then gasping
Woman's loud cry: "Help me"
Woman crying
Loud knocking
Deafening crash, as of building collapsing

BREAKFAST AND BED

BY AMY FOX

BREAKFAST AND BED was first produced in the Ensemble Studio Theatre Marathon of One Act Plays in 2006. It was directed by Abigail Zealey Bess. The cast was as follows:

ELOISE .... Karen Young
LEX .... Julie Fitzpatrick

BREAKFAST AND BED

A small apartment — living room/kitchen. Eloise, late thirties, very attractive, is at the kitchen table, drinking coffee and smoking a cigarette. She wears a silk robe and her hair is in a towel turban. She is looking at Lex, late twenties, who is asleep on the couch, half dressed in clothes from the night before. A pair of black boots are in the middle of the floor. Lex opens her eyes. She sits up, covering herself and looking around, disoriented.

ELOISE. Hi.
LEX. Oh — hi.
ELOISE. Coffee?
LEX. Oh, no thanks.
ELOISE. It's good coffee. Hazelnut. If you like that.
LEX. I'm okay, thanks. I was just looking for ... Chris.
ELOISE. There's orange juice.
LEX. That's okay. Um, is Chris here.
ELOISE. No. There's bagels ... Chris had to go to work.
LEX. Oh.
ELOISE. We have that cream cheese, mixed with lox.
LEX. I'm okay — um, so Chris is —
ELOISE. At work. I could give you the number, if you want.
LEX. Um, okay. Sure.
ELOISE. I gotta look for it. I should have it memorized, but it's just one of those that doesn't stick, you know. You sure you don't want some coffee? Or a cigarette?
LEX. Okay, some coffee. *(Eloise pours a cup of coffee and sets it down, instead of handing it to Lex. Lex sits down at the table.)*
ELOISE. That's right. A person's got to relax. Enjoy the morning. That's the way to live. Enjoy the night, enjoy the morning.
LEX. Sure.
ELOISE. Did you?

LEX. What.

ELOISE. Enjoy your night.

LEX. Yeah, it was ... pretty good. So, roommates?

ELOISE. Sorry?

LEX. You and Chris are roommates?

ELOISE. Sure. I guess we are. As it were.

LEX. She didn't say.

ELOISE. Well, here we are. How's the coffee?

LEX. Good, thanks.

ELOISE. So let me guess. You went to one of those cat places, what is it called, the pussy cat something or other ...

LEX. No —

ELOISE. Nanny's.

LEX. Lee's.

ELOISE. Oh yes, Lee's.

LEX. Have you been there?

ELOISE. No, what's it like?

LEX. I don't know. It's small, crowded, but kind of cute. Red velvet drapes, that kind of thing.

ELOISE. Like a lounge.

LEX. Yeah, in the back.

ELOISE. Good music?

LEX. Yeah, loungy kind of.

ELOISE. In the East Village, right?

LEX. Yeah, Fifth Street. Right next to that vintage store, Roses?

ELOISE. I like that place. A couple months ago, I found this incredible flapper dress there. Red, with a fringe.

LEX. I love those. I always thought in a previous life, maybe I was a flapper.

ELOISE. Absolutely. What fun. And you have those big eyes.

LEX. Thanks ... *(Eloise holds out the coffee pot, offering more to Lex.)* Thanks. *(Eloise pours the coffee.)*

ELOISE. So was it crowded? Lee's? Oh, you said it was. It's just I really haven't been out to Lee's, or the pussy cat place, so I'm just curious. How it works, what goes on.

LEX. Yeah, it was pretty much my first time. At Lee's, I mean.

ELOISE. Oh.

LEX. So I wasn't really sure how it would be. But mostly it's just a bar, you know. I mean that's what it is — a bar. You should check it out, if you want.

ELOISE. Do people dance, or just hang out.

LEX. Both, pretty much. We danced.

ELOISE. Chris? Really?

LEX. Yeah.

ELOISE. Huh.

LEX. What?

ELOISE. Oh, no, it's just she doesn't always feel like it. Or so she says.

LEX. Oh.

ELOISE. But, what do I know. I wasn't there.

LEX. Well, we … danced.

ELOISE. Sounds good. Chris didn't say much this morning, but she never does. Seems like she usually has a good time, she always seems to meet people. *(Lex takes this in, not sure how to react.)*

LEX. … Do you have that number?

ELOISE. I'm surprised, actually, now that I think about it. I mean, don't take this the wrong way, but you don't seem like her … type.

LEX. Well. Look, I don't know what your whole setup is here, but —

ELOISE. I mean, you said it was your first time, right, at Lee's?

LEX. Sure, but —

ELOISE. Are you … straight?

LEX. What?!

ELOISE. I'm sorry, she pretty much does her own thing, Chris, but I look out for her. Somebody's got to.

LEX. She seems like she could look after herself.

ELOISE. All I'm saying is, I know some people go through a kind of phase, a time of exploration…

LEX. Look, I don't know you —

ELOISE. Which is fine, I just think if that's what it is, just leave Chris out of it. That's all I'm saying. Because she doesn't need that. To wake up next to a straight girl.

LEX. Well, she didn't wake up next to anybody, did she. Because she went to WORK or wherever, and actually I'm feeling a little weird about this whole thing so could you just give me that number.

ELOISE. I mean you're cute, that's not what I meant, when I said her type, you've got those beautiful flapper eyes. What I meant was …

LEX. What?

ELOISE. Never mind. Let's just have some breakfast.

LEX. I don't want breakfast.

ELOISE. Coffee then.

LEX. I don't want coffee. I want to go home and take a shower. I just want Chris's phone number.

ELOISE. Okay. Hang on. *(She gets up and starts going through a pile of papers. Lex gets up and follows her, waiting for the number.)* How old are you?

LEX. Twenty-six.

ELOISE. She's a baby. Twenty, did you know that?

LEX. No.

ELOISE. What did she tell you.

LEX. Twenty-six.

ELOISE. And you believed her?

LEX. I don't know.

ELOISE. She plays tough, but she's a baby. That's why I worry about her. Don't want to see her getting mixed up in some iffy situation. Somebody who doesn't know what they're looking for.

LEX. Look. I'm just gonna leave my number. And I don't know if you'll give it to her, but whatever. *(Lex grabs a sheet of paper and scribbles down her number.)*

ELOISE. Of course I'll give it to her. Why wouldn't I give it to her.

LEX. Look, I have no idea what the deal is here.

ELOISE. You think I would do that? Confiscate your number?

LEX. You might.

ELOISE. Well then, you'd better take hers. Just in case. I think it's in here. *(She dumps out the contents of her bag. A photograph of a little girl in pigtails is among the items.)* There she is. Little sweetheart.

LEX. That's Chris?

ELOISE. Four years old.

LEX. You carry that around?

ELOISE. Wouldn't you? Look at that face.

LEX. Okay look, I have to ask you, are you guys a thing? I mean what's the deal.

ELOISE. A thing?

LEX. You and Chris?

ELOISE. Oh! No —

LEX. Because — There's this very weird vibe —

ELOISE. Hold on, there's no vibe, because …

LEX. Oh yes there is —

ELOISE. No — because —

LEX. What —

ELOISE. ... I'm her mother.

LEX. What?!

ELOISE. It's true. She's my little girl. She moved home in December.

LEX. Home.

ELOISE. I don't know, she got dumped by some guy...

LEX. Some guy?

ELOISE. It happens.

LEX. Yeah, guys happen. But she doesn't like guys —

ELOISE. Not so much, it turns out.

LEX. I'm sorry, but I'm just a little disoriented. She said she was twenty-six, and this was her place, and —

ELOISE. Well, adjust.

LEX. What?

ELOISE. I mean, for god's sake, you knew her for, what, six hours? So not everything she told you is what you thought, fine, adjust. Integrate the new information.

LEX. Integrate.

ELOISE. That's what our brains do with new experiences.

LEX. Yeah, well, there's a little too much integration going on right now. Too much information to...

ELOISE. Right. I guess you're still processing last night. *(Silence. Lex finally stands up.)*

LEX. I'm gonna go. Yeah. I'm gonna do my processing somewhere else.

ELOISE. I'm sorry. I shouldn't have ... you don't have to go.

LEX. Yeah, well, just tell Chris ... I don't know.

ELOISE. You still want the number? ... I understand. I'll tell her ... it's not her, can I tell her that, that it's because of ... me. Or is it you.

LEX. It's really just ... it's none of your business.

ELOISE. You're right.

LEX. I mean none of this is your business.

ELOISE. I'm sorry — I guess I just thought you might want to talk to somebody.

LEX. To you?

ELOISE. No, of course not. I mean I'm sure you have lots of people to talk to.

LEX. Yeah — sure.

ELOISE. I'm sure as soon as you're through that door you'll have your cell phone out ready to call whoever …

LEX. Yeah, it's really great, because whoever — always takes my calls. Always. Which is really great. If you do want to talk to somebody.

ELOISE. …Would you like some more coffee? You can stay a few minutes. We don't have to talk, we could just have some coffee. If you want. *(The phone rings. Eloise answers it.)* Hello? Hi, Ted. Oh, sure. Um yeah, that would be — okay. As long as it's funny, right? Never mind. I was kidding, or something. Sure, seven o'clock, bye. *(She hangs up.)* I have a date tonight. He wants to go to stand-up comedy. You're still here.

LEX. I guess I'm still … integrating.

ELOISE. Take your time. Here. *(She pours more coffee. Lex slowly sits down.)* It's not very romantic, stand-up comedy, is it? Chris hates it. Really hates it. Did she tell you that? Well I guess she didn't tell you much. You thought she was twenty-six.

LEX. She seemed … mature.

ELOISE. Well, a lot can happen to a girl before twenty. I had Chris when I was eighteen. *(She sees the phone number among the items from her bag.)* There it is. The elusive work number. And here's ours. *(She scribbles the numbers down.)*

LEX. She works where? She said, last night, she was an architect.

ELOISE. She's the assistant to the assistant to an architect.

LEX. Ah. *(She picks up the phone number.)*

ELOISE. Do you think you'll call her? After all this? I mean she's not the type to wait by the phone, but I'd like to give her some clue what to expect …

LEX. I don't think I should make any promises.

ELOISE. So you won't.

LEX. I don't know. I didn't say that. I said —

ELOISE. Come on, it's pretty clear. I just think it's only fair to be honest about things. I mean it's your decision — no one is saying you have to call, but —

LEX. Look. I have a boyfriend.

ELOISE. Oh.

LEX. I mean not entirely.

ELOISE. I see.

LEX. We're taking some time. So I can figure some things out.

42

ELOISE. Right. You did strike me as…

LEX. I'm trying to figure some things out.

ELOISE. Such as … if you like girls.

LEX. Pretty much.

ELOISE. How do you figure that out?

LEX. I'm not sure.

ELOISE. I'm always wondering how this happens.

LEX. I'm kind of taking it one day at a time. And I haven't really told anyone what's going on.

ELOISE. I thought you were looking for someone to talk to. I just had that feeling.

LEX. I don't know. I guess I thought last night would give me some kind of clarity.

ELOISE. Did it?

LEX. We were drunk — it's a blur. And a night like that can't just change everything, can it?

ELOISE. It would have to be a pretty special night.

LEX. George — that's my boyfriend — he's very logical — wants to analyze the situation from every angle. He's coming back to town tomorrow, from a job interview. Has to decide whether to move to Houston. He wants me to tell him where we stand. He asked me to do something definitive before he came back. Definitive.

ELOISE. I think about this a lot. How you would know. I mean I'm curious, as a mom. And just in general. Chris just rolls her eyes, when I try to ask her.

LEX. I don't know. Maybe for some people it's easier.

ELOISE. Chris first kissed a girl when she was thirteen. Then she started kissing boys. Till she met Julie. That was her first love, I think. She's been through four girlfriends and two boyfriends — I think she uses the guys, really, for vengeance. But I don't know. I look at her and I don't know what to say. I don't know how to talk to her. Her world is so much bigger. But I want to understand it.

LEX. At least you try. I could never talk to my mom about anything. And she never really cared to ask.

ELOISE. I always wanted a daughter who would tell me everything. I just assumed I'd have some clue what she was talking about.

LEX. So you grill the girls she brings home. Is that usually what happens around here?

ELOISE. First time. It's just, I have so many questions. Everything is so wonderfully complicated these days. I don't know what my life might have been if I had that kind of freedom.

LEX. Well, I'm sure you could …

ELOISE. Yeah. You think there's still time?

LEX. … Why not.

ELOISE. You're very brave.

LEX. Brave?

ELOISE. To just jump out there and test the waters. I don't even know your name.

LEX. Lex.

ELOISE. Eloise.

LEX. So … who's your date with. Tonight.

ELOISE. Ted. Third date. He's fine. Chris doesn't like him, says he smirks.

LEX. Does he?

ELOISE. Yeah.

LEX. Well, I hope you have a good time…

ELOISE. You know something? I don't want to go. He's boring. I hate stand-up comedy. And he's boring. There, I've said it. I'm totally bored. Jesus. I haven't been on a good date in a year! Jesus.

LEX. *(Laughing a little.)* I'm sorry …

ELOISE. It just gets worse and worse. The Teds, and those are the sweet ones. The assholes are worse. That's it. I'm not going.

LEX. Really?

ELOISE. I shouldn't go, right?

LEX. Well if you don't like him…

ELOISE. That's it. I'm not going. We decided.

LEX. We did?

ELOISE. You're a lifesaver.

LEX. Okay.

ELOISE. Do you think I'm gay?

LEX. What?

ELOISE. Chris thinks so. I know she does. She's always dropping hints. She wants to know why I'm never dating anyone I like. And why I ask her so many questions all the time …

LEX. And why you end up having breakfast with some girl she brought home?

ELOISE. I don't like eating alone … What?

LEX. Nothing. So these questions you're always asking Chris …

ELOISE. What it's like. How it's different, how it feels different.

44

LEX. I think it depends on the people.

ELOISE. Well of course it depends on the people! I'm not so thick as that. But I want to know — I mean, for you, for example, how does it feel to ...

LEX. To ...

ELOISE. Kiss someone. A girl. A woman.

LEX. I'm not sure if I've kissed a woman.

ELOISE. Oh.

LEX. But hypothetically, probably it would feel like...

ELOISE. Like? *(They look at each other. Lex kisses Eloise — a tentative kiss.)* Why did you do that?

LEX. I thought you wanted me to.

ELOISE. Did you want to?

LEX. Yes.

ELOISE. It's the same, isn't it. Chris always said it felt the same, but I didn't believe it. But don't you think?

LEX. No, I don't. Not that time.

ELOISE. Oh. I don't know. Maybe it's different. *(They kiss again, still tentatively. The phone rings. They break away. The phone rings again and again, the answering machine picks up.)*

CHRIS. *(On the machine.)* Hi Mom, it's me. I'll be home like at five. Oh, and sorry about this morning — the girl — I know that was totally weird. *(A beep, then silence.)*

ELOISE. We can't do this.

LEX. I know.

ELOISE. It's too —

LEX. Yeah. I mean, Chris —

ELOISE. She's my daughter —

LEX. I should probably go.

ELOISE. Yeah. I guess that would be ...

LEX. I'll just ... put on my boots. *(Lex struggles with the boots, while Eloise watches, perturbed. The phone rings again. Eloise can't decide whether to answer it. The machine picks up.)*

TED. *(On the machine.)* Hi Eloise, it's me. Ted. I don't know if you recognize my — well, it's me, anyway, Ted. So the comedy group, I know you were wondering about their reputation, they're called the Flying Buttresses, I know it's a weird name, but my friend says they're totally hilarious. In, like, a quirky way ... *(Eloise reaches over and turns off the machine.)*

LEX. I'm sorry.

45

ELOISE. *(Sadly.)* For what?

LEX. I don't know.

ELOISE. Then don't be. *(The phone rings again, a couple of times. Finally Eloise grabs it.)* Ted? Hi. This is not a good time. *(She hangs up. She starts to laugh, but quickly stops, a pained expression on her face.)*

LEX. Okay. Well, okay. Bye.

ELOISE. Um — did you ever get the phone number?

LEX. For Chris? At work?

ELOISE. Or for here.

LEX. I kind of — don't think I'll call.

ELOISE. Yeah. I'll tell her. Not to ... wait for anything.

LEX. Okay ... bye. *(She goes, awkwardly. Eloise looks defeated.)*

ELOISE. Bye.

End of Play

PROPERTY LIST

Cigarettes
Coffee cups
Coffee pot
Black boots
Pile of papers
Paper and pen
Handbag and contents, including photo of child and piece of
paper with a phone number written on it
Red flapper dress

SOUND EFFECTS

Phone ring
Answering machine beep
Answering machine — Chris message
Answering machine — Ted message

CELL

BY CASSANDRA MEDLEY

CELL was produced in the Ensemble Studio Theatre Marathon of One-Act Plays in June 2011. It was directed by Jamie Richards. The cast was as follows:

RENE .... Lizan Mitchell
CERISE .... MaConnia Chesser
GWEN .... Shyko Amos

CHARACTERS

RENE —African-American woman, 50

CERISE — Rene's sister, African-American, 45

GWENDOLYN — Cerise's daughter, African-American, 23

PLACE

Flint, Michigan. The living room of René's mobile home.

TIME

Summer 2011.

CELL

Scene 1

Rene's trailer. Early evening sound of outside door opening, door chimes. Rene enters and immediately runs offstage into another room.

Cerise and Gwen enter. All are dressed in the same uniform: dull tan short-sleeved shirts and green pants.

Gwen is operating a cell phone video camera, pointing it at herself and Cerise.

GWEN. *(Into the cell phone camera speaker.)* "Here we are back home, after our first day on the job."

CERISE. *(Re the camera.)* Daughter, honey. Baby, that's enough, now. That's your auntie's, you can't just use it up.

GWEN. Just wanna show us coming home after our first day at work. *(Rene runs on, holding a small chocolate cake, with a balloon on a string that reads "WELCOME.")*

RENE. WELCOME HOME, EVERYBODY! *(They all hug. Gwen kisses Rene on the cheek.)*

GWEN. Ahhhhh! WONDERFUL! Thank you, so much!!

CERISE. *(Delighted.)* Sis! Ain't you so sweet!! You didn't have to! *(Gwen continues videotaping with the cell phone.)*

GWEN. *(Into the cell phone.)* And here's Auntie's cake she got for us!

CERISE. My big sis is the very, very best. *(Rene playfully waves this off.)*

RENE. Girl, get outta here with all that! Family is family. *(Gwen continues filming.)*

GWEN. Auntie, your trailer's so nice.

RENE. It's a roof over my head.

CERISE. Don't wanna crowd you — if you ever need, y'know, complete privacy, Gwen and me can go to the mall for a few hours.

RENE. Let's get the blankets out 'fore we're too tired.

CERISE. Tonight, I'll take the corner. Gwen, you sleep on the love seat.

GWEN. Momma, you need the love seat for your back. Corner's fine with me.

CERISE. *(To Gwen.)* We not here to freeload off your aunt. I want us serving her every chance we get, understand?

GWEN. Of course, I understand.

RENE. Relax, Cerise, this not no boot camp.

CERISE. Sis, I'm making us some meatballs and spaghetti for tonight. You got bath salts? Gwen, go in the bathroom, find bath salts, make a hot tub for your aunt. *(To Rene.)* All the standing you do on your feet. *(Gwen suddenly turns and videotapes the badge on her sleeve. Cerise turns and "politely" snatches the cell phone away from Gwen, handing it to Rene.)*

RENE. *(To Cerise.)* Ah, give her a break, let her 'lone. *(Rene hands Gwen back the camera.)*

CERISE. *(Exasperated, re: the badge.)* All damn badge say is, "Thurston Corporation."

GWEN. I now work for Thurston Corporation Immigration Detention Center.

RENE. It's the first real job she's ever had. Nothing wrong with being proud.

CERISE. Rene, what can I getcha? As I recall, you like great big glasses of ice cold lemonade filled to the brim with ice …

RENE. You wanna pour me a gin and tonic, that'd be great. Better still, hold the "tonic." *(Rene winks at Cerise, who is very surprised.)*

RENE. *(Laughing at Cerise's shock.)* Baby Sis, if you looking for Rene of ten years ago, you looking for a mirage. *(Gwen turns camera on herself, speaks as if being interviewed. Cerise and Rene exchange amused glances.)*

GWEN. *(Into camera lens.)* How do I feel after my first day, at "Thurston Corporation"? Great. I feel great. I never knew there were so many immigrants from so many places. And Momma's working there, too.

RENE. *(To Gwen.)* Tell on that phone how you was promoted to the front desk, right away.

CERISE. *(To Gwen.)* Now, that *is* something to crow about.

Promoted to the Front Desk on the very first day! *(To Rene.)* Sister, I'm so glad I broke down and — and —

RENE. "Hello"? What'd you think, I was gonna let you be sleeping on the streets back in Cleveland and starve to death?

CERISE. *(To Gwen.)* You didn't put that on camera?! *(Gwen puts the cell phone down, with an irritated expression.)*

GWEN. *(To Rene.)* Child, when my unemployment run out, I thought "Hello, welfare." Then they come talking 'bout I don't meet the regulations. I said to that woman, I said, "So what we supposed to eat, air?" Don't tell me God's works ain't wondrous!

RENE. Remember now. Always look sharp. Keep in mind that "our kind" is always on the radar with upper management.

CERISE. Girl, ain't that the truth! They never wanna give black folks a break.

RENE. *(To Cerise.)* Why should they? If we gotta work twice as hard as anybody else, I say, so be it. Builds character. Have no time for excuses. *(To Gwen.)* I may be a supervisor, but I also *got* a supervisor, know what I'm saying?

CERISE. Leon Banks. We understand. She understands. *(To Gwen.)* Auntie's taking a big risk in hiring us.

RENE. Never mind that.

CERISE. *(To Gwen.)* Don't forget it.

RENE. Why would she forget it?

CERISE. *(Cheerfully to Rene.)* Least we come cheap for Thurston — don't have to worry 'bout no union workers or — paying benefits …

RENE. Sh-h-h! Never mention that, understand?! Never. To nobody.

CERISE. Of course, of course, *(Trying for a joke.)* This trailer ain't "bugged," is it? *(Serious.)* You don't gotta worry about us, we your family.

GWEN. *(To Rene.)* All them folks in the waiting room? They trying to get to they families locked up inside. Right?

CERISE. Never you mind. Just do your job.

RENE. *(To Gwen.)* Sister, I'm getting thirsty. *(Cerise runs off. Rene places a gentle arm around Gwen.)*

RENE. What are your front desk responsibilities? *(Gwen speaks in a studied tone.)*

GWEN. Man the front desk on the shift I'm given. Make all visitors stay in the line and in order … keep the waiting room calm.

RENE. Good. Very good.

GWEN. Waiting room be so packed.

RENE. If they keep they seats like they should, they'll fit. Thing is for you to keep order whenever you're assigned to the front desk. *(Cerise yells from offstage.)*

CERISE. That's right!

RENE. Otherwise, we'd have a madhouse. *(Cerise enters with a tray — hands Rene her drink, hands Gwen a can of soda.)*

CERISE. A madhouse. That's exactly right.

RENE. Good. Remember, now, Leon likes you. Took one look at ya, and said "front desk."

CERISE. *(To Gwen.)* Ain't that something?! And he's the supervisor over your auntie! *(Rene tosses back her drink. Cerise is shocked.)*

RENE. Trouble is ...

CERISE. *(Alert.)* Trouble? What trouble? *(Rene strokes Gwen's cheek.)*

RENE. Baby, I'm not criticizing, alright? *(Gwen nods, curious.)*

RENE After all, it was just your first day. I understand that.

CERISE. What'd she do? She punched the right buttons on the computer, didn't she? *(Rene just centers on Gwen.)*

RENE. I'm the visitor coming to the window. "I want to see Maria Conchita Elena Gonzalez!" Here's you ... *(A too soft, mousy voice.)* "Step away from the window, please. Please, step away. From the window ..."

CERISE. *(To Rene.)* Oh, she gotta BOOMING voice when she wanna use it. Just wait till you hear her BOOMING. *(To Gwen.)* Remember, now, you're seated behind plate glass. *(Rene studies Gwen.)*

RENE. Twenty-three years old. All grown up.

CERISE. And ready to USE that BOOMING voice.

RENE. *(To Gwen.)* Okay, I'm the visitor — what's the first thing you do?

GWEN. Get the name, then check the computer screen to see if they got clearance to visit the resident.

RENE. Which, nine times out of ten — they won't have. Or the person they wanna see'll have been moved out.

GWEN. Moved to where?

CERISE. *(To Rene.)* Girl, I'm just so thankful I finally broke down and called you when I did.

GWEN. *(Booming voice.)* STEP AWAY FROM THE WINDOW! WAIT YOUR TURN! *(Cerise and Rene clap.)*

GWEN. *(To Rene.)* The people living behind the locked door. Where they sent to when they moved out?

CERISE. Is that our business?! NO, IT IS NOT.

RENE. *(Admonishing Cerise.)* Don't talk to her like that. *(Then to Gwen.)* They flown back into the wide world. Wherever they come from in the first place. That way we get to have our country to ourselves.

GWEN. But ...

CERISE. Lookit you! My daughter doing a service for her country.

GWEN. What about all them waiting room families left behind?

RENE. *(Pause, then.)* It's complicated. *(Gwen whirls on Rene.)*

GWEN. I'm not retarded!

CERISE. Is that how you speak to your Aunt? *(Claps her hands.)* Okey-dokey ... Who's ready for spaghetti in about a half hour?

GWEN. STEP AWAY FROM THE WINDOW! WAIT YOUR TURN!

RENE. Terrific. And if they don't wanna be patient and start screaming and hollering or threatening, then what??

GWEN. Press the button. Let the armed guards handle the situation.

RENE. Excellent. Remember, you're behind plate glass. You're protected.

GWEN. STEP AWAY FROM THE WINDOW. WAIT YOUR TURN. STAND IN LINE! *(Rene and Gwen nod, impressed, smiling. Rene opens her arms wide.)*

RENE. Welcome to my lil' "hideaway."

CERISE. Spaghetti coming up!

Scene 2

Rene's trailer — the next night

The "Welcome" balloon dangles, still bouncing in the air.

All three sit with dinner trays on their laps and empty plates, having finished their meal. They are in their bras, their work pants still on.

Rene and Cerise soak their bare feet in small basins. Rene has a shot glass on the floor next to her feet.

Rene holds the TV remote and channel surfs, various program sounds come from the unseen TV on the invisible wall. Gwen speaks into the cell phone video camera.

GWEN. "Day Two at Thurston Corporation. How do I feel? Very good." *(She clicks off the phone and refers to a stack of brochures in her lap. She slowly turns the pages, reading. Holds up brochure.)* Thurston Corp. Head Office is located way, way off in Houston, Texas. They got Thurston places in ten states! *(Gwen watches Rene with admiration. Pause, then.)* Auntie, ten years away from you, is too long.
RENE. Well, we all together, now. *(Cerise clears the plates.)*
CERISE. *(To Gwen.)* Momma gonna save up enough money, we'll get our own trailer, give her back her privacy. *(Cerise disappears off with the plates. TV plays, Gwen reads.)*
RENE. What about stayin' here with me?
GWEN. Thurston's number three in the nation. *(Cerise returns with towels. She hands a towel to Gwen, who wipes her feet dry, still reading the brochures. Cerise stops cold, smiles.)*
RENE. *(To Cerise.)* Thought you always wanted to go to community college. Use your savings for that.
CERISE. Girl, that old pipe dream done gathered ten years' worth of dust. *(Cerise kneels down and proceeds to wipe Rene's feet dry. Rene*

snatches her feet away.)

RENE. *(Embarrassed.)* Cerise! Now, no call for you to be — *(Cerise grabs Rene's feet and continues wiping and massaging them.)*

CERISE. *(Playful.)* Hush up. You the one been standing on your toe jams for twenty-some years, me and Gwen only have had two days …

RENE. Sister, you could take a criminal justice course over at er … uh … uh … *(Snaps her fingers to help her memory.)* Gilmore Community — *(Gwen holds up brochure.)*

GWEN. Ain't that something, Momma? "Third in the nation."

CERISE. *(To Rene.)* Tell ya what I "got" — and it's thanks to you. A job. A job that'll go on and on and on, that's what I "got." Long as there's foreigners getting caught without their papers, me and you, and Gwen here won't never be laid off. Now, I call that way more "real" than taking some chance on some Community College. *(To Gwen, playful.)* What you think about it, Baby? *(Gwen holds up brochure.)*

GWEN. The rooms they got pictured here are just "rooms." See? There's no jail bar on a window or on the front of the cell.

CERISE. Gwen, Momma said for you to let that go. Rest ya eyes and get some rest! *(Cerise snatches the brochures from off Gwen's lap.)*

RENE. *(Playful.)* Who's ready for cake, raise ya hand!

CERISE. Sister, sing pretty like you used to! Let's hear you hit them notes. Gwen, wait till you hear this. *(To Rene.)* You oughta go back to church and sing in a choir, like when we was coming up. *(Rene "playfully" waves this away.)*

RENE. Oh, stop.

GWEN. I think I DO remember … Auntie sounding like a song-bird.

CERISE. Soprano. *(Rene sips from her shot glass, notices Cerise's disapproval.)*

RENE. Ha. Don't be so cross-eyed.

CERISE. Now, you remember my own tribulations with that. *(Pause, then.)* Sing to us, like you used to! *(Gwen and Cerise wait on Rene, her smile drops.)*

RENE. *(Quite serious.)* I said *drop* it! *(Silence, Cerise and Gwen stare at Rene.)*

RENE. *(Motioning to Gwen.)* Leon Banks is sweet on our girl. *(Gwen is totally shocked by this news. Rene nods to Gwen.)*

RENE. That's right, that's what he tole me.

CERISE. *(To Gwen, pleased.)* Leon! Your supervisor!

RENE. He thinks she cute. Specially with that lil' round behind she carrying around.

GWEN. Gross.

CERISE. You ain't got to marry the man. Just smile at him once in a while.

RENE. After all, you're twenty-three.

CERISE. 'Bout time somebody started circulating around. That's what happens with normal girls, only natural.

GWEN. Pleas-s-s-se … He's like 35, or something. AND with that gut.

CERISE. Appearances are only skin-deep. *(Gwen holds up the brochures.)*

GWEN. How come these pictures don't show the real cells in that place?

CERISE. We talking 'bout something important to your whole life. Who the hell cares 'bout some damn photos? Talk sense.

RENE. *(To Gwen.)* Leon's unmarried. Well. Divorced.

CERISE. *(Even more delighted.)* And since you're starting fresh, he wouldn't have to know nothing about, where you come from before.

RENE. He's clean living. Well-mannered. Strong in the Lord.

GWEN. Well, I ain't.

CERISE. Don't say that. Come Sunday, we going straight to some altar, somewheres, getting down on our knees, and thanking Jesus.

RENE. *(To Gwen.)* Let him take you to the movies.

CERISE. She certainly will. *(Pause.)* He won't be "trying" nothing?

RENE. He ain't no "dog" like some of these running 'round here. *(Gwen holds up the brochure.)*

GWEN. Reading this, you'd never know that it was a "momma-baby" jail.

RENE. *(Very calm.)* Sweetheart, they not in no jail.

GWEN. But —

RENE. They're in a *Residence* until they can be returned to they countries of origin.

GWEN. Baby cribs in the jail cells, what else can you call it?

CERISE. Gwen, are you hired to judge? Is that your job description?

RENE. Looks kinda weird, I know. But that's only 'cause you're not used to it. Wait till you've been around a couple months. *(Pause.)* Remember, it's all supervised. We use government guidelines. You see how we have a lil play yard for the kids …

GWEN. That itty-bitty cement square is a yard for the kids?

CERISE. *(To Gwen.)* Do *you* want your own children someday? Well?

GWEN. Yeah, guess so.

CERISE. And a husband with a good job, and a nice, big house to live in? Answer!?

GWEN. Well, who don't want that?

CERISE. Okay, then. Focus on that, and leave the Department of Homeland Security in the hands of the Department of Homeland Security.

GWEN. I'm just trying to teach myself what my job is.

RENE. Uh-huh, well, one of the most important parts of the job is to let go when you get home at night. Let go of the day and, like your momma says, focus on your own life.

CERISE. Hello?!

RENE. And I certainly hope you won't be asking Leon none of this nonsense. Or anybody else on the job.

GWEN. I know better than that.

CERISE. She knows better than that!

GWEN. I'm not "dumb."

RENE. 'Course you not. You're like anybody else. *(Cerise takes the TV remote.)*

CERISE. Let's see the *Oprah* rerun for today.

GWEN. All I'm saying is like, "wow"... I mean ...

CERISE. *OPRAH* Y'ALL!

GWEN. I mean, like, what would that be like to have to take a shower with no shower curtain every day ... *(Cerise and Rene concentrate on the TV.)*

CERISE. *(To Gwen.)* Sh-h-h-h — *(To Rene, pointing to the screen.)* Oh, she just got on white women and they diets ...

RENE. *(To Cerise.)* Turn on *Judge Brown* — he usually got our folks fighting over something. *(Silence. Cerise and Rene watch the TV.)*

CERISE. *(Pointing to screen.)* Now, lookit that hair on her head! Ump-ump-ump!

GWEN. What it feel like to have lights out just 'cause we say "lights out," to have to eat whatever we give you, like it or not? And you can't take ya baby for a stroll ... and ... you don't talk English, so you don't understand ... and ... all the clanging all the time ... and the howling, plus the babies crying ... and the disinfectant smell mixed in with dirty diapers ... families visit, but the immigrants be behind glass — They can't touch them, they can't hug them, nothing. *(Rene switches off the TV, turns to Gwen. Cerise glares at Gwen.)*

GWEN. I'll go brush my teeth. Be all ready for tomorrow. *(Gwen makes to exit.)*

RENE. Niece. *(Gwen whirls around, frightened.)*

GWEN. No more questions! Promise! *(Silence. Gwen and Cerise wait in apprehension.)*

RENE. I got a slinky short silver nylon dress. Fit me fifteen years ago. Still in style. You can wear it on your date. *(Cerise claps in relief.)*

CERISE. *(To Rene.)* Like I say, what would we do without you?! *(Rene and Gwen lock eyes.)*

RENE. Sweet dreams. *(Rene exits to her bedroom.)*

Scene 3

Third night.

Rene sits. Gwen stands over her with an electric hot comb. Gwen is pressing or refreshing Rene's hair. R&B music from radio.

RENE. Your momma sure 'nough loves that hot shower don't she? *(Gwen instantly yells offstage.)*

GWEN. MOMMA, GET OUT THE SHOWER SO OTHER PEOPLE CAN USE IT! *(Gwen continues to comb Rene's hair.)*

RENE. How come Starbucks and McDonalds didn't work out back in Cleveland?

GWEN. Orders come in so fast at them places ... customers start yelling. *(Pause.)* I really like living here in Flint, Michigan. *(Gwen continues pressing Rene's hair.)* How come, you and Momma let ten years go by without speaking?

RENE. Child, there's so much blood under the bridge 'tween me and y'momma ... you don't wanna dip a toe in it, believe me.

GWEN. You was always letting me snuggle on your lap. that's what

I'll never forget. *(Pause.)* How come I always been slower than other girls my age? *(Rene strokes Gwen's face.)*

RENE. Nonsense. How could you be slower if you're learning to speak Creole?

GWEN. Huh?

RENE. "Huh?" *(Rene strokes Gwen's face, then suddenly tightens her hold on Gwen's arm.)*

RENE. I'm hearing that you learning to speak French and Spanish. Guess you'll start up on A-rab talk, next, huh? *(Gwen attempts to pull away from Rene, who holds her tight.)*

RENE. You must think I'm a fool. You think I'm a fool?

GWEN. Whatsamatter??

RENE. *("Sadly.")* What we gonna do with you? You're supposed to be our flesh and blood.

GWEN. I … I'm doing everything just like you told me..

RENE. Naw-naw, you going around speaking French, Spanish or patois, or whatever the hell it is — that's what you doing! *(Cerise appears, dressed in a bathrobe, smiling, is about to speak, then backs into shadows, watching Gwen and Rene.)*

GWEN. I'm following orders, just like you've told me.

RENE. You got "orders" to speak to cell #293? Or cell #156? *(Cerise steps forward.)*

CERISE. What is all this? *(Cerise pulls Gwen from Rene's grip.)* You hurting her. *(Rene "calmly" centers on Gwen.)*

RENE. Don't you realize they got cameras all through that place? Think, Gwendolyn, think!

CERISE. Don't be talkin' to her like that …

RENE. *(To Gwen.)* Everywhere you turn there's a lens watching us AND "them" breathe, swallow, piss, and take a shit.

CERISE. Hold up! Leon told me Gwen is doing a terrific job …

RENE. Sure! Till he caught sight of her on camera, sneaking a chat with Cell 293! That Haitian woman. She's holding her baby up to the bars on her cell, so Gwen here, can pat the baby's head!

CERISE. What?

RENE. Yep. Y'know the one we hadda put in isolation? We got a close-up of Gwen here! *(To Gwen.)* Tell her, Gwen!

GWEN. Her name's Marie-Louise.

RENE. It's *not* your job to know what her name is.

GWEN. I was just saying hi.

RENE. You was stroking that Creole woman's baby's head…!

TELL HER. And the Mexican? Gwen, here is sharing her curried chicken leftovers with the Mexican. We got it live on camera! *(Cerise turns to Gwen.)*

CERISE. You know that's way, way against regulations.

GWEN. The Haitian baby may have a fever …

RENE. Doctor comes second Friday of every month. The momma's been given a cold compress to use. Meanwhile, only reason you gonna get *one* more chance is 'cause Leon thinks you gotta sweet ass! Otherwise, he would've kicked you out this afternoon. He's got his own supervisor!

CERISE. Tell your auntie you ain't gonna never do this again.

GWEN. Me and Marie the same age. But she got a baby she gotta keep in jail.

RENE. *(Pause, then to Gwen.)* When ya "new friend" is put on the plane back to Haiti, guess you wanna go to the shanties, too? Or go with ya Mexican back to the filthy hovels there, see how well you enjoy it!

CERISE. Okay, okay … no need to be so rough. She won't do it no more. No need to climb the walls about it …

RENE. Weren't for me, you two wouldn't *have* no walls!

CERISE. What you want? Huh? Me groveling on me knees in gratitude? Would that be enough?

GWEN. Momma, don't. She's right. I was wrong. I apologize.

RENE. Girl, it gets to be where these "apologies" ain't nothing but breath in, and breath out. *(Cerise dramatically falls to her knees.)*

CERISE. *Thank* you, Sister, for all your kindness.

RENE. Well, I'm *sorry,* but am I to — to — to always be your "Red Cross" for the rest of my natural life?

CERISE. I ain't asked you for nothing in ten years.

RENE. Right, and *when* you do call — it's 'cause you ain't got a pot to piss in, or a window to throw it out, or a front, or back yard to soak it up!

CERISE. Least I don't feed on bitterness 'cause my dreams didn't work out.

RENE. Cerise! I'm NOT gonna end up on the unemployment line just 'cause your daughter's brains was marinated in moonshine! *(Rene's hand flies up to her mouth as if wanting to take back this slip. Gwen glances from one to the other.)*

CERISE. She don't mean nothing by that. Do you, Rene.

RENE. Niece, only job security I got is my rep for following orders. This ain't Never-Never Land where life just gives me this trailer to live in 'cause God is good and Jesus Christ done had a Second Coming.

GWEN. I won't do it no more. I promise.

CERISE. She means it, Rene. *(Rene focuses on Gwen.)*

RENE. Sit. We do not speak to them in the cells, and we do not let them speak to us. It's for they own good. DO NOT FRATER-NIZE. You do that, you get the "boot" before you can sneeze. *Never* get the immates' hopes up, chaos would break out. The rules are for the good of everybody. You think you helping your Creole and Mexican ladies by befriending them? *You are not.*

GWEN. Yes, ma'am. *(Cerise attempts to embrace Gwen, who backs away from her.)*

CERISE. Momma will help you.

RENE. We do not find out about them, we do not let them find out about us. We do not answer their questions. We do not ask them questions. We do not get involved!

GWEN. We do not get involved.

RENE. Hidden camera don't lie, and my home don't come free.

GWEN. Yes, ma'am.

RENE. And as far as you concerned: don't wanna hear no Creole, no Mexican, no South American, no A-rab, or nothing else coming out of your mouth.

GWEN. I'm gonna be so much better tomorrow. *(Gwen goes to Rene in supplication, she reaches to embrace Rene. Rene holds back, then returns the hug after a pause. Cerise crosses over and embraces them both. Lights cross fade.)*

Scene 4

Gwen enters, her shirt untucked and slightly disheveled. She is obviously upset. She lays across the couch, takes out a joint and puffs on it for a few moments. A sustained beat ...

Rene and Cerise enter, dressed as just coming from work.

CERISE and RENE. What in the world...? Where you been?! We been looking all over for you!

GWEN. *(Mocking.)* Hitched a ride with Leon. *(She holds up the joint, mocking.)* He give me this to "calm my nerves." *(Then to Rene.)* That's right, LEON.

RENE. Now, look here — It was nobody's fault.

GWEN. That's Leon over and over: "It was nobody's fault."

RENE. He's absolutely right. It probably had a special condition before the momma even came here ...

GWEN. "It?"

RENE. Don't you get all up in my face. Y'know what I'm trying to —

GWEN. Patrice! The baby's name was *Patrice.*

CERISE. We all know that.

GWEN. Now y'all got a tiny corpse on ya hands. Yesterday, his little head ... felt so hot ... now his teeny body bundled up like a package ... little Patrice..

RENE. *(Shocked.)* The morgue is off limits.

GWEN. Not if I let Leon cop a "feel" on my booty, it ain't. *(Cerise moves to slap Gwen, Gwen ducks.)*

CERISE. Gwendolyn, that's enough.

GWEN. Only acting like a "normal" girl, y'all. Hold up, I don't gotta act normal, I was "marinated."

CERISE. Rene, don't let her speak to me like that.

RENE. *(To Gwen.)* We realize it was hard for you to be put through this ...

GWEN. Me? Me!? *Hard* for me? The momma's name is Marie-Louise! And now her Patrice is sealed up in a white sack.

RENE. Oh, for heaven's sake. I got folks I have to deal with week after week, month after — I been working for Thurston for twenty-seven years!

GWEN. Marie-Louise. Now put on a plane ... *(Pause.)* In her lap, her baby's ashes.

CERISE. She'll have the comfort of her family.

GWEN. *(Bitter.)* Her flesh and blood, huh, momma? Huh, auntie?

RENE. Don't be giving me no "evil eye," girl! Babies get sick sometimes without nobody knowing why. It happens.

GWEN. Thought they got cameras trained on everybody night and day?

RENE. I should NEVER have talked myself into putting you on staff.

CERISE. *(To Rene.)* Now, don't say that.

GWEN. I bet wrapped-up dead babies is a regular thing in that place. One doctor once a week — get sick on the wrong day, tough.

RENE. Only thing "regular" is you not doing what you was told.

GWEN. I've done EXACTLY what you —

RENE. Surely you not raising your voice to me?

CERISE. *(To Gwen.)* Back off, girl. *(Gwen grabs a brochure off the table, holds it up, starts ripping it to shreds.)*

GWEN. It ain't shit!

RENE. Alright, it's sad! But they know the risks they take when they take the risk of trying to come here, and trying to stay without documentation. They *know* this! They break the law and want *us* to feel bad for 'em and take the blame!

GWEN. No wonder you got insomnia.

RENE. Now you can slant ya snake eyes at me all you want, but this the real world, Gwen. And every time you put a piece of pie to your lips, or curl up in ya warm blanket at night — Thurston Corp. is paying for it.

GWEN. Or "was." I'm fired, right? Right? *(Rene avoids Gwen's glance.)*

RENE. Depends.

GWEN. You mean, if I keep my mouth shut, I still got a job.

RENE. In all fifty states, the unemployed are overflowing the streets.

CERISE. *(To Gwen.)* You're a normal person. Hear me? And like any normal, everyday, ordinary person, you gonna just go, day to day, and do what you gotta do to get by. *(Gwen runs off. Silence as the two sisters hold a stare.)*

CERISE. She'll settle down. After while.

RENE. *(Pause.)* I know. I'll tell Leon to *really* "romance" her. Gifts, flowers, dinner. Y'all can't stay here without her income.

CERISE. I know, I know. We understand. *(Gwen enters, bringing out her duffle bag piled with random clothes.)*

CERISE. Uh-uh. Where do you think you're going?

GWEN. *(To Rene.)* You faked my name on the witness form, didn't you?

RENE. Think how many piles of job applications Thurston gets day in, and day out.

GWEN. *(To Rene.)* You signed *my* name ... saying that yesterday, I felt no fever coming from off that Haitian baby.

RENE. DAMN STRAIGHT I SIGNED FOR YOU. And I volunteered to do it, too.

GWEN. I should have screamed and hollered yesterday, and got some help to come to that cell.

RENE. When will you finally begin to understand that it's your life, or theirs — and no in-between? *(Cerise attempts to steer Gwen.)*

CERISE. *(To Gwen.)* You turn right around and put that stuff back, and get ready for bed.

GWEN. Gotta be some joint in this town that'll need floors scrubbed in exchange for a meal. Maybe they'll lemme sleep in the celler.

RENE. *(To Gwen.)* Patrice? Lemme tell you about your little Patrice. He was born a bottom feeder just like you..

CERISE. Rene, please ...

RENE. Just like me and ya Momma and everbody in this broken down town, and all the ton of nobodies that crowd up the bottom pit of this world. And there ain't no "Abra — ca — da — bra" that's gonna change that.

GWEN. Even a fucking ghost town like this gotta have a Salvation Army ... *(Rene grabs Gwen and drags her to the window, Cerise panics.)*

CERISE. Rene!

RENE. *(To Gwen.)* See how dark it is out there? See? Vacant lots, and everybody's locked up inside they place. See them pitbulls chained up over there? Bars on they windows, just like bars on my windows — to keep out the thugs. *(Points.)* See that van cruising by? They wolves on the prowl, licking they chops, with they fangs drooling, and out for prey. You'd be a sweet, tasty morsel.

CERISE. *(To Rene.)* You her auntie! Talking to her like that!

RENE. *(To Gwen.)* Go on out there, looking at me with that evil eye like that! Since I offend you so much! See if you make it to the end of that lamp post! Go! Get out!

GWEN. Gonna have that dead baby in my dreams from now on.

RENE. Dreams go up in smoke eventually. *(Beat.)* Believe me.

GWEN. I thought you were my guardian angel.

RENE. *(To Gwen.)* Girl, you, and ya momma was in the Cleveland Greyhound with benches for a bed, and the stinky winos and crack hos surrounding you! Who'd she call "collect"? Me! You wanna goddam happy ending, then take your ass to the movies!

GWEN. *(To Rene.)* I can't stand to look you in the face.

RENE. I know my life is less then dust. But do you hear me whining and complaining? No, you do not. Do you hear me blaming anybody, or gnashing my teeth, or wailing at God? "God how come you made me at the bottom of the heap!" Nonsense. If I'm to be a grain of sand in this goddam world, then I'm a grain of sand. This is how I must live, and so I live. I take it, and I take it, and I take it. That's right, and I'm gonna keep on taking it … and taking it … and taking it … and TAKING IT … *(Rene starts to break down.)* Keep on. And on and on and keep … keep … keep keep! *(Cerise reaches out to embrace Rene.)*

CERISE. Sister.

RENE. DON'T YOU MUTHERFUCKING "SISTER" ME, GODDAMMIT! Gwendolyn, you turn on that TV! *(A long moment as they lock eyes. Gwen does not move. Finally, Cerise snatches up the TV remote, switches on the TV. Rene and Cerise sit, staring into the TV screen.)*

CERISE. *Desperate Housewives,* y'all! *(Gwen stands in place not moving. She looks towards the door for a moment, turns back, drops her backpack to the floor. Lights fade to black.)*

End of Play

PROPERTY LIST

Cell phone with videocamera
Small chocolate cake
"Welcome" balloon on string
Tray with drink, can of soda
Dinner trays, empty plates
Small foot basins
Shot glass
TV remote
Stack of brochures
Towels
Electric hot comb
Joint
Duffel bag and clothes

SOUND EFFECTS

Door opening
Door chimes
TV program sounds
R&B music from radio

DIVERSIONS

BY CHRISTOPHER DURANG

AUTHOR'S NOTE

This is a very old play of mine. I hesitate to tell you how old. Shall I tell you? Maybe later. Well … I wrote it in 1967, when I was eighteen. My freshman year at Harvard College I put on a production of it in the Loeb Experimental Theater. After that, I went into a two-and-a-half-year depression and did nothing else until 1971.

One reason I felt an impulse to include this play is that it was the first thing I wrote that started to be in "my style."

For some reason I had written plays for most of my youth. I wrote my first one — a brief version of *I Love Lucy* — when I was eight. After that, I wrote short plays every year. Once I wrote a play called *Dinner at 8* based on the title alone. At that point I hadn't seen the Kauffman-Hart play.

With Kevin Farrell, a school friend who composed music, I started to write musical comedies. The first one, written when he and I were thirteen, was called *Banned in Boston*. It was extremely innocent and precocious, and ended like a Shakespearean comedy with four marriages. (Its subplot had to do with two conservative aunts trying to shut down a local show they found "offensive;" odd foreshadowing, given the protests my play *Sister Mary Ignatius Explains It All for You* eventually received, including in Boston.)

Banned in Boston was performed at Kevin's and my all-boys Catholic high school. The administration "borrowed" girls from a local girls' Catholic school. The priests at my school thought the show was fun, but the nuns at the girls' school were offended by a number where one of their girls dropped a shoulder strap seductively. (Clearly, they didn't relish an homage to *Gypsy*, as I did.) That girls' school vowed not to loan out girls for plays at my school again.

Our second musical, when we were fifteen, was getting a bit more cynical and was called *Businessman's Holiday*. (We borrowed girls from another school and had no trouble.) It ended with the heroine realizing the hero was a jerk, turning down his marriage proposal, but otherwise seemed very much like an imitation of a "commercial" musical from the '50s.

Diversions, for what it's worth, seemed to come from a different place in me. It has a young person's existentialism, I guess; it is also drawn to absurdism, which I seemed to know from Edward Albee's *The American Dream* and maybe from some Fellini movies.

So, hoping it's worth reading, here's DIVERSIONS.

DIVERSIONS was presented at the Loeb Experimental Theater at Harvard College in Cambridge, Massachusetts, in the fall of 1967. It was directed by the author. The cast was as follows:

MAN .... Chris Durang
NUN .... Pat Pilz
ALOYSIOUS KAIN .... Mike Stone
POLICEMAN 1 .... Ernst Louis
HYSTERIA .... Bonnie Raitt
POLICEMAN 2 .... Lynn Stephens
JUDGE .... Burton Craig
CLERK .... Richard Bock
DEBORAH KAIN .... Jane Stein
PROSECUTING ATTORNEY .... Dean Sheppard

(Note: Bonnie Raitt is indeed the same person who went on to become the much-enjoyed singer-composer. She was good as an actress, too.)

CHARACTERS

MAN, who's feeling depressed

NUN, who's not depressed and is very sure of herself

ALOYSIOUS KAIN, a bit of a milquetoast

POLICEMAN 1

HYSTERIA, who screams a lot

POLICEMAN 2

JUDGE, who's a bit irritated

CLERK, who's trying to do his best

DEBORAH KAIN, Aloysius' sultry wife

PROSECUTING ATTORNEY, who's virile, knows his place in the world

DIVERSIONS

Scene: A man is standing at the edge of a small platform, preparing to jump. A Nun enters right. She sees him and screams. The Man almost loses his balance because of her scream.

NUN. Don't jump! *(The Man looks at her, then prepares to jump again. The Nun repeats her scream; then rushes up to him and pulls on his arm.)* Don't jump!

MAN. *(Tired.)* Why not?

NUN. It's against the fifth commandment. *(The Man struggles to free himself from her grasp and to attempt jumping again.)* Don't jump! *(The Man looks at her.)* Think of your wife.

MAN. My wife left me five years ago.

NUN. Think of your children.

MAN. I did. *(Vaguely sarcastic.)* And I appreciate your concern, but please leave me alone. *(He prepares to jump again.)*

NUN. *(In a booming voice.)* If you do that, you're going to go straight to Hell. *(The Man glares at her, starts again.)* DON'T JUMP!

MAN. *(Exasperated, getting angry.)* My good woman ...

NUN. I'm not a woman, I'm a nun.

MAN. My good woman, would you kindly go away and let me be in peace! *(He throws off her clutching hand. She seethes.)*

NUN. Who do you think you are? Who do you think you are, to speak to me that way? How very typical of our modern secular world you are. Someone tries to help you, to reach out, and you turn on them, tell them to leave you in peace. Well, I'm finished helping you, I'm finished with you completely. As a matter of fact, I'll help you jump. I'll push you. *(She rushes toward him; they struggle. From left enters Aloysius Kain, a New York Times under his arm. Seeing the trouble, he raises his newspaper and charges over.)*

ALOYSIUS. Hey! Stop that. Stop that at once. *(He starts to pull the Nun away from the Man.)*

NUN. Help! Let go!

ALOYSIUS. Stop this! Stop this! *(A policeman enters, sees the three people struggling. he blows his whistle.)*

MAN. *(Amidst the struggling.)* If you'd all just leave me alone. *(The policeman struggle to pull Aloysius off the Nun; Aloysius tries to pull the Nun off the Man; and the Man tries to keep his balance. Suddenly through a quick motion, the Policeman loses his balance and falls off his platform, lying in a lump on the floor. [The Policeman, not the platform.] A scream offstage. Aloysius, the Nun, and the Man stare aghast at the body at their feet.)*

MAN. He fell.

ALOYSIUS. My God.

NUN. Do you think we're … murderers?

ALOYSIUS. Don't say that. *(Enter an Hysterical Woman with another Policeman.)*

HYSTERIA. I saw it! I saw it! They pushed the policeman over. I saw it! *(She gives an ear-splitting scream.)*

ALOYSIUS. *(Nervous.)* For God's sake, woman, not so loud.

NUN. *(Frightened.)* She's a liar! We didn't push that man over. *(She points to to Aloysius.)* He did.

ALOYSIUS. I did! How can you say that? You saw me. I didn't do anything I was trying to … *(The Hysterical Woman screams again. As the above commotion has been going on, a Clerk has entered, carrying a desk, followed regally by the Judge. The Clerk drags the dead body of the first policeman off the stage. The Judge sits behind the desk. The second policeman ushers the group [Aloysius, the Nun, the Man, and the Hysterical Woman] over to the Judge. Much noise and commotion.)*

JUDGE. *(Rather tired.)* What is it? Be quiet, please. I can't think.

COP. Your Honor, these three people have been accused of murdering a policeman.

JUDGE. *(Looks at the people in front of him.)* Which three people?

COP. *(Pointing to Aloysius, the Nun, and the Man.)* That woman and the two men.

JUDGE. *(To the three.)* How do you plead?

ALOYSIUS. Not guilty.

MAN. Not guilty.

NUN. Clergy. And I demand to be tried in an ecclesiastical court. *(The Judge frowns.)*

JUDGE. *(To the Cop.)* Who is the other one?

COP. She is the witness. *(The Hysterical Woman screams very loudly,*

followed by a series of sobs. The Clerk rushes in with a pair of pants.)
CLERK. Here are your pants, Your Honor.
JUDGE. *(Distracted.)* What?
CLERK. Here are your pants.
JUDGE. *(Checking.)* But I have my pants.
CLERK. I don't know. The dry cleaners just sent them, that's all. *(Clerk exits. The Judge puts pants on desk.)*
JUDGE. *(To Hysteria.)* And what did you see, my good woman? *(Hysteria, terrified, breaks down into further sobbings.)*
HYSTERIA. *(In between sobs.)* I demand to call my lawyer.
JUDGE. *(Truly exasperated.)* I can't understand her.
MAN. She said she wants to call her lawyer.
JUDGE. Very well, Clerk! Bring in a telephone. *(Enter the Clerk with telephone and another pair of pants.)*
CLERK. Here are your pants, Your Honor.
JUDGE. I have my pants. *(The Clerk looks sternly at him.)* Oh, very well. I won't argue. *(He takes pants, gives telephone to Hysteria. Exit Clerk. Hysteria, calmer, picks up telephone. Silence. She starts to cry again.)*
JUDGE. Now what's the matter?
HYSTERIA. I don't have a lawyer. Everyone else has a lawyer but me. *(Her sobbing is making her talk unintelligible again.)* I'm only a simple working woman ... *(Etc.)*
ALOYSIUS. I don't see why she needs a lawyer. We're the ones who need a lawyer.
HYSTERIA. *(At climax.)* But he's trying to intimidate me!!
JUDGE. My good woman ... *(Hysteria gives a horrifying scream.)*
COP. Your Honor ...
JUDGE. I'm sick of this case. I want nothing more to do with it. It's disgusting.
COP. But Your Honor ...
JUDGE. Clerk! Clerk! *(Enter the Clerk.)* My pills, quickly.
CLERK. Which ones?
JUDGE. Ulcer, liver, and kidney. *(Motioning toward the Hysterical Woman.)* And please take this woman out. I'm going to rest. Court recesses for my pills. *(To Clerk.)* Tell the Prosecuting Attorney I want to see him when he comes. *(Exit Judge left.)*
CLERK. *(To the Nun.)* I tried to contact your Mother Superior but she was praying.
NUN. You needn't have done that. I have God. I could levitate

right up to the ceiling if I wanted.

CLERK. *(To the Man.)* I wasn't given any number to call for you. Do you want to call anyone?

MAN. No.

ALOYSIUS. Did you call my wife?

CLERK. Yes. She's coming down here any moment. Alright. All of you wait in the other room until court begins again. Come on. *(Clerk leads everyone offstage right. Moment's pause. Enter Deborah Kain, Aloysius' wife. She stands alone on stage, take out her compact. She arranges her hair and powder. Enter the Prosecuting Attorney. They stare at one another, somewhat startled. The Prosecuting Attorney then exits right. Enter the Clerk.)*

CLERK. You are the wife of Aloysious Kain?

DEBORAH. Yes.

CLERK. I'll send him in to you. *(Exit Clerk. Enter Aloysius. Silence.)*

ALOYSIUS. Nice of you to come.

DEBORAH. *(Rather loudly.)* I got a phone call which said you were being held for murder. Are you, Henry?

ALOYSIUS. Why did you call me "Henry?" You know my name is Aloysius. Have you been seeing Henry again?

DEBORAH. I've asked you not to pry into my personal life.

ALOYSIUS. Have you?

DEBORAH. Now, Aloysius. Don't badger me. *(Silence. Aloysius looks away uncomfortably. Deborah takes out a cigarette, waits for him to light it.)*

ALOYSIUS. I'm sorry. I don't have my lighter with me. *(She puts away the cigarette, disgusted.)* Are you going to stay for the trial or go to your bridge club?

DEBORAH. Bridge club was called off today.

ALOYSIUS. Oh. Well, I guess I'll wait in the other room. *(Deborah stares vacantly into nowhere. Aloysius exits. Enter the Prosecuting Attorney.)*

ATTORNEY. You're one of the defendants' wives, aren't you?

DEBORAH. Yes.

ATTORNEY. *(Close to her.)* I'm the Prosecuting Attorney. *(They kiss.)*

DEBORAH. Henry … darling. *(Breaks away.)* We must be careful not to be seen like this. Aloysius doesn't approve.

HENRY. I like the new shade your hair's dyed. *(He lights her cigarette. She begins to pace.)*

DEBORAH. Henry, just think. Now that Aloysius has been arrested, we can get married. And if he gets the electric chair, I won't have to leave the Church. *(Silence.)*

HENRY. You didn't tell me you were Catholic.

DEBORAH. I didn't think it really mattered.

HENRY. It does.

DEBORAH. But why? Henry. You're not ... predjudiced, are you?

HENRY. Well, I wouldn't want my daughter to marry a Negro.

DEBORAH. Who would? But are you predjudiced against ... Catholics? *(Henry turns away.)* Henry, what a horrid thing to come between us. Henry, please. Believe me. I haven't been to Church for years, except for Christmas. And I'd even give that up for you.

HENRY. It wouldn't matter. It would be a blot on our past.

DEBORAH. Henry, does this mean we're through. *(He refuses to turn towards her. She begins to sing softly.)* We kiss in a shadow, we hide from the moon, our meetings are few ... *(He turns and they embrace. They kiss.)* I didn't know you had a daughter.

HENRY. I don't. I was speaking figuratively.

DEBORAH. Oh. *(They kiss again. Enter the Nun, the Man, Hysteria, the Clerk, and Aloysius. Upon seeing the kissing couple, Hysteria gasps. Henry and Deborah break away, startled. The Nun goes to the couple, pulls them apart.)*

NUN. Are you married?

DEBORAH. Take your hands off me.

NUN. God have mercy on your souls. *(Enter the Judge. Hysteria screams.)*

JUDGE. Is she still screaming?

ALOYSIUS. *(Humiliated, angry.)* Deborah, this is the end of us.

DEBORAH. Aloysius, don't be dramatic.

ALOYSIUS. You are incapable of love.

DEBORAH. Then why did you kill that policeman if you didn't think he was my lover? *(She sits down triumphantly. Hysteria stands up and applauds. The Clerk enters and admonishes her, slapping her palms. He give the Judge a pair of pants. Exits.)*

ALOYSIUS. I didn't kill the policeman!

JUDGE. Order in the court. Who is the Prosecuting Attorney?

HENRY. I am.

JUDGE. Oh yes. I spoke to you a moment ago. And the Defense Attorney?

ALOYSIUS. Your Honor, this thing is so simple, I will defend myself. It can be all over in a minute. Now you see, I saw this nun *(He points.)* trying to push this man off the roof, and I came to stop her. Then a policeman came along, and apparently thinking I was trying to push the nun or both of them off, came and joined the struggle. By mistake, one of us pushed him off. *(Silence.)*

JUDGE. That is the most preposterous story I have ever heard in my life.

DEBORAH. Aloysius! Tell the truth. *(To the Judge.)* He thought the policeman was my lover, while the Prosecuting Attorney here really is.

ALOYSIUS. That's a lie!

HENRY. No it's not. I am your wife's lover.

ALOYSIUS. I know that. I mean, it's a lie that I thought the policeman was my wife's lover.

JUDGE. Oh, so you admit that the policeman was not her lover. Then what possible reason could you have for killing him? *(Pause. Everyone stares ar the Hysterical Woman.)* That's funny, I could've sworn you were going to scream. *(Hysteria smiles at him. Henry suddenly stands.)*

HENRY. I call to the stand the prosecution's first witness, the eye witness. *(Hysteria comes to the stand, terrified. Silence. Henry begins to shout.)* And did you not see that man, Aloysius Kain, willfully push that policeman off the roof, while that horrified couple over there watched aghast? I put it before you, did you not!?

HYSTERIA. *(Screaming.)* I did! I did!

HENRY. And did you not see that innocent couple try to stop Mr. Kain from this horrible murder?

HYSTERIA. *(Screaming.)* YES!

HENRY. *(Abruptly stopping shouting.)* Your witness, Mr. Kain.

JUDGE. *(Not hearing; out of it.)* What did you say?

HENRY. I said to Mr. Kain that if he should like to cross-examine the witness, he might do so. *(Judge nods.)*

ALOYSIUS. *(Standing.)* My good woman …

HENRY. *(Shouting.)* Objection! Your Honor, he is browbeating the witness! *(To Hysteria.)* Isn't he?

HYSTERIA. *(Anguished.)* YES!

HENRY. She can no longer stand it. Can you?

HYSTERIA. NO! *(She breaks down wildly.)*

JUDGE. Clerk! Clerk! *(Enter the Clerk. He takes Hysteria out.)*

HENRY. Your Honor, I submit that we rid those two people over there, the nun and the man, of any charge. It is obvious that they had nothing to do with the policeman's murder.

JUDGE. Quite obvious.

ALOYSIUS. But Your Honor …

DEBORAH. Aloysius. Don't involve two innocent people. Don't!

JUDGE. *(To Nun and Man.)* You may go.

NUN. Thank you, Your Honor. *(To Aloysius.)* I shall pray for your soul. *(Exits.)*

MAN. *(Starting to leave, but turning back.)* Your Honor, this man didn't …

JUDGE. Shush. My head. Wait — do you play bridge?

MAN. Yes. Sometimes.

JUDGE. Good. And you, Mrs. Kain?

DEBORAH. I am one of the best players in my bridge club. I'd be at my bridge club today if one of the members hadn't killed herself.

JUDGE. What an inconvenience for you. And you, Mr. Prosecuting Attorney?

HENRY. Indeed I do, Your Honor.

JUDGE. Good.

ALOYSIUS. *(In a small voice.)* I play bridge.

JUDGE. The defendant is never allowed.

ALOYSIUS. Oh.

JUDGE. Clerk! *(Enter the Clerk.)*

CLERK. Yes, Your Honor?

JUDGE. What? No pants?

CLERK. I forgot them in the other room.

JUDGE. Well, never mind. Bring me a pack of cards instead. *(The Clerk produces them from his pocket.)* I presume Mr. Kain will not mind if we play bridge to make the trial go faster.

ALOYSIUS. I don't think it's fair, Your Honor.

JUDGE. That was meant as a statement, not a question. *(The Clerk exits. To the other players.)* I'll deal.

DEBORAH. *I'll* deal. *(She takes the cards and deals at the Judge's desk. They are seated thusly: right to left, the Man, the Judge, Deborah, and Henry. The Man looks at Aloysius, then away. Deborah is finished dealing — sloppily. They arrange cards.)*

HENRY. Your Honor, I suggest that since we have heard all the evidence, we send the jury out for a verdict.

JUDGE. My God! I knew there was something I'd forgotten. There is no jury.

DEBORAH. Well then, make the decision yourself.

JUDGE. Oh. Alright. Who bids first?

HENRY. I do. One club.

MAN. I pass.

JUDGE. You're supposed to say two clubs.

MAN. I pass.

JUDGE. You're supposed to say two clubs. *(Deborah kicks the Man under the table.)*

MAN. I pass, I said. *(The Judge twists the Man's wrist. Deborah kicks the Man under the table.)*

JUDGE. Say two clubs. *(The Judge, Henry, and Deborah begin to chant together.)*

JUDGE/HENRY/DEBORAH. Two clubs, two clubs, two clubs ...

MAN. TWO CLUBS! *(The three laugh, go back to their places.)*

DEBORAH. Good. Start over.

HENRY. One club.

MAN. Two clubs.

JUDGE. Three clubs.

DEBORAH. Four clubs! *(Judge, Deborah, and Henry laugh, clap their hands in glee.)*

ALOYSIUS. Your Honor ...

HENRY. Objection!

JUDGE. Contempt of court.

DEBORAH. Judge, the verdict.

JUDGE. *(Looking up from his cards.)* Oh, yes. *(Shouts at Aloysius.)* The court has come to the decision that you are guilty. Sentence: death! Clerk! *(Enter the Clerk, with a pair of pajamas.)*

CLERK. Your pajamas, Your Honor.

JUDGE. So I see. Clerk. Execute Mr. Kain, please. *(Aloysius does not move. The Clerk take a gun from the Judge and shoots Aloysius. No one looks or moves except the Man. The Clerk then drags the dead body off.)*

MAN. I think I'll quit.

JUDGE. No you don't.

DEBORAH. Henry, darling. Now that Aloysius is dead, we can get married. Your Honor, can you marry us?

JUDGE. I can do anything. Do you, Henry, take this wo ...

HENRY. I do.

JUDGE. Do you Mrs. Kain ...

DEBORAH. I have already, but I will again.

JUDGE. I pronounce you man and wife. You may kiss the bride.

(Henry and Deborah kiss very coldly.)

JUDGE. May I kiss the bride?

DEBORAH. Certainly. *(Deborah and the Judge kiss passionately.)* Let's play bridge.

JUDGE. Alright.

DEBORAH. *(Looking at her cards)* Let's start over. I don't like my hand.

HENRY. Deborah, what about a honeymoon?

DEBORAH. *(Shouting.)* If you're going to nag me, I won't let you play with us. Judge, I want a new fourth.

JUDGE. Very well. Clerk! *(Enter the Clerk.)* Do you play bridge?

CLERK. Very well indeed.

JUDGE. Then come play with us. *(Clerk sits down where Henry was.)*

HENRY. But Deborah, what about me?

DEBORAH. What about you, Aloysius? *(Silence. Henry is shaken.)*

HENRY. *(Correcting her.)* Henry.

DEBORAH. Henry. Sorry. *(Looking at her cards.)* Four spades.

CLERK. Pass.

MAN. Pass.

JUDGE. Pass.

DEBORAH. *(To Man.)* You're dummy.

MAN. I know.

HENRY. *(Shouting.)* DEBORAH! WHAT ABOUT ME? *(Deborah does not hear him; no one does, except the Man; and he turns away.)*

HENRY. Deborah, answer me!

DEBORAH. *(To Man, who keeps looking back at Henry.)* You're not concentrating.

MAN. Bridge makes me sick. *(He turns his back to all of them.)*

HENRY. DEBORAH! *(Deborah hands him a revolver from her purse. Henry shoots himself.)*

JUDGE. How many hearts are out?

DEBORAH. *(Gaily.)* All of them. *(Putting down her cards.)* I'm tired of bridge. What other games can we play? *(They all put down their cards.)*

JUDGE. I don't know.

CLERK. *(Discreetly.)* There's always double solitaire.

JUDGE. But there are three of us. Only two people can play that.

DEBORAH. Clerk, why don't you play it with me?

CLERK. Alright.

DEBORAH. We can play it in your room so we won't be bothered. *(The Clerk, carrying the Judge's pajamas, starts to exit with Deborah and the cards.)*

JUDGE. But Deborah, wait! What about me? What about me? *(Deborah and the Clerk, dragging the dead Henry out after them, are followed by the Judge, who keeps calling after them. They exit. The Man is now alone on stage. He gets up from his chair, looks about him. He arranges the chair next to the desk, and then climbs up onto the desk. He looks down to the floor. He prepares to jump. Enter the Nun.)*

NUN. *(Sternly.)* Don't jump. *(The Man looks at her very seriously. She remains stern, uncompromising. He sits down on the desk.)*

MAN. *(Barely audible.)* Why not? *(To the floor, more or less.)* Why not, why not, why not ... *(His voice trails off. He just stares at the floor.)*

End of Play

PROPERTY LIST

New York Times
Police whistle
3 pairs of pants
Telephone
Compact
Cigarette
Lighter
Pack of cards
Pajamas
Gun
Revolver

THE GREEN HILL

BY DAVID IVES

THE GREEN HILL

Jake stands alone in a pool of light.

JAKE. I just have to close my eyes. If I close my eyes (I said), I'm there, I'm on the green hill. Actually on it. Walking right up the side of it. I probably go up there every other day, for a second or two. I've been doing it for years. *(Lights have broadened to reveal Sandy.)*

SANDY. And what is this green hill?

JAKE. I don't know.

SANDY. Is it a memory?

JAKE. It's as real as a memory. I feel as if I've really been on that hill sometime. But I've never gone to anyplace that's like it!

SANDY. And now you can go to this green hill anytime you want.

JAKE. Anytime I want (I said), and Sandy said …

SANDY. Okay …

JAKE. Okay, Sandy said. Go to it now.

SANDY. Go to it now. Go to the green hill.

JAKE. I just have to close my eyes. Give me a second. *(He closes his eyes and keeps them closed through the following.)* And … Okay. I'm there.

SANDY. You're on the green hill?

JAKE. I'm on the green hill.

SANDY. Am I on it with you?

JAKE. I don't know … Somehow you are … No, I'm all by myself up here. Just like always. *(Breathes in deeply.)* God, the air up here! And I can feel the grass underneath my shoes. Very soft, very springy.

SANDY. Is the hill high?

JAKE. It doesn't feel very high … not like a mountain. It could be a hill in the Swiss Alps, below the big snowcapped mountains.

SANDY. You've never been to the Swiss Alps.

JAKE. I've never been anywhere. Except up here.

SANDY. So what do you see up there?

JAKE. It's always the same. I'm pretty close to the top, angling up the slope toward my left. The hill's a little too steep to walk straight up. *(Points, his eyes still closed.)* The top's right up there, not very far. Maybe fifty more paces and I'll be on top of the hill.

SANDY. What's on the top?

JAKE. Nothing. Just the green hilltop, and then blue sky.

SANDY. Are there any trees?

JAKE. No. No trees. No rocks or stones. Nothing.

SANDY. Buildings?

JAKE. Just grass. It's like a lawn, very smooth. Deep green. Like pasture. Pale blue sky. Maybe a few very thin clouds. The air very fresh, slightly cool. It's like a morning in spring. Maybe seven o'clock, before anything's happening, and I'm just out here walking. God, it's wonderful up here!

SANDY. Are there any sounds? Birdsong? What do you hear?

JAKE. Nothing. Just the breeze.

SANDY. What's behind you, at the bottom of the hill?

JAKE. I don't know. I'm looking upwards, toward the top.

SANDY. Look back now. Turn around and look back down the hill. *(Pause.)*

JAKE. I can't. I'm looking the other way. *(Points up before him at an angle.)* That way.

SANDY. Have you ever gotten to the top?

JAKE. No, I'm always right here on the hill, same place, just below the top, angling up to my left.

SANDY. If you ever got to the top, what do you think you'd see?

JAKE. I don't know. I don't know. I'm just out walking.

SANDY. In the middle of nowhere.

JAKE. Complete nowhere. And I never feel so free. It's not how it looks up here so much, it's that I never feel so free as when I'm up here. And all I have to do is close my eyes. God...!

SANDY. And if you open them...?

JAKE. *(Opens them and looks at her.)* I'm back. Hello.

SANDY. Hello. Welcome home. You look refreshed.

JAKE. It is refreshing up there.

SANDY. Color in your cheeks and everything.

JAKE. It's always like a mini-vacation.

SANDY. So what is this green hill? Someplace you went as a kid?

JAKE. I never went anywhere like that as a kid. Or since, that I know of.

SANDY. Someplace where you had a traumatic experience?

JAKE. I don't feel traumatized up there.

SANDY. Not yet.

JAKE. Not yet.

SANDY. Maybe this is a dream you had.

JAKE. It feels too real. It's real, Sandy. It's real. It's a real place.

SANDY. Okay.

JAKE. It's not a dream.

SANDY. Money?

JAKE. Money ... ?

SANDY. It's a big heap of green and you're free and happy up there. Maybe it's a vision about having a pile of money.

JAKE. No. It's not like that.

SANDY. Sorry.

JAKE. It's palpable, and real, and specific.

SANDY. Well, I wish *I* had a green hill ...

JAKE. I wish I had a green hill, she said, and I said, Come up on mine.

SANDY. How do I get up there?

JAKE. I don't know (I said). But do you love me anyway?

SANDY. I love you anyway.

JAKE. Will you make love with me anyway?

SANDY. Anyway. But if you close your eyes and go to the green hill, I'll kill you. *(Sandy exits).*

JAKE. Then one day I'm walking down the street and I pass a travel agency. *(A poster flies in, a picture of a plain green hilltop against a plain blue sky, and just the word "TRAVEL.")* And there it is. The green hill. My green hill. *(Travel Agent enters.)* "Excuse me," (I say).

TRAVEL AGENT. Cancún, or Club Med?

JAKE. Neither one. That poster in your window.

TRAVEL AGENT. Acapulco.

JAKE. No, the other one, the green hill. Do you know where that place is? Where that picture was taken?

TRAVEL AGENT. No idea. The Land of Travel. *(Travel Agent starts out.)*

JAKE. I'll buy a ticket to wherever it is (I say), if you'll help me find out. Is there anything written on the back?

TRAVEL AGENT. *(Checking the back of the poster.)* Nothing on it. Sorry.

JAKE. What'll you take for the poster?

TRAVEL AGENT. We are not in the poster business.

JAKE. I'll give you ten bucks.

TRAVEL AGENT. You can't take a *bus* anyplace for ten bucks.

JAKE. Fifty. A hundred. What do you say?

TRAVEL AGENT. Travel is a little more complicated than you think. *(Travel Agent exits and Sandy enters.)*

SANDY. *Two hundred dollars?*

JAKE. It was cheap.

SANDY. And that's the green hill.

JAKE. That's it.

SANDY. Your green hill.

JAKE. Definitely. So it exists! The green hill is real!

SANDY. And you've been, what, channeling it all these years?

JAKE. Who knows?

SANDY. How can you tell it's your specific green hill?

JAKE. I just know.

SANDY. It's lovely. A little generic, isn't it?

JAKE. No! Not at all!

SANDY. If it really was your green hill, wouldn't you be in this picture? Right about … here, walking up the side, angling toward the left…?

JAKE. Very funny.

SANDY. No. I think it's terrific.

JAKE. But look here, on the edge. You see the small print?

SANDY. There's always the small print.

JAKE. "Photo by Kretchmar."

SANDY. Kretchmar.

JAKE. Find Kretchmar and I find the hill. The real hill. I get to really stand on it, go to the top, see what's around it. Look at the view.

SANDY. That would be true.

JAKE. And guess what? *I found Kretchmar.*

SANDY. So where's the hill?

JAKE. Well, it's a little more complicated than that … *(Sandy remains as Mrs. Kretchmar enters. She and Jake speak as if into telephones.)*

MRS. KRETCHMAR. *(Accent.)* Yes, my husband took that picture. I remember the poster. It says "Travel."

JAKE. Can I speak to Mr. Kretchmar?

MRS. KRETCHMAR. I'm afraid Morgan died two years ago.

JAKE. I'm sorry. Is there any way you could tell me where he took that picture? Or maybe the company that produced the poster, would they know?

MRS. KRETCHMAR. It's a little more complicated than that.

JAKE. What if I come to you?

MRS. KRETCHMAR. You don't want to do that.

JAKE. What's your address? I'll come see you and we'll talk.

MRS. KRETCHMAR. Well, all right, if you really want to ... *(Mrs. Kretchmar exits.)*

SANDY. So where does Mrs. Kretchmar live?

JAKE. Finland.

SANDY. Finland. Why am I getting this Hel-sinking feeling?

JAKE. Do you want to go to Finland?

SANDY. Not unless I can take it as a personal day.

JAKE. Sandy ...

SANDY. I know this is important to you.

JAKE. We could take a cheap flight. It'd be fun.

SANDY. It's not only the money.

JAKE. You have responsibilities.

SANDY. "Morgan Kretchmar." Is that even a real name? Is that a *Finnish* name? They probably lure unsuspecting people to the tundra, rob them of everything they have, and dump their bodies in the Baltic.

JAKE. You said you wanted to know what the green hill was like.

SANDY. Jake, I can't

JAKE. Okay. Okay.

SANDY. Do you love me anyway?

JAKE. I love you anyway.

SANDY. Will you make love with me anyway?

JAKE. How do you say "yes" in Finnish?

SANDY. You tell me. When you reach the finish line. *(Sandy exits. The poster flies out. Mrs. Kretchmar enters with a portfolio.)*

MRS. KRETCHMAR. Here are some examples of my husband's photos.

JAKE. Fantastic.

MRS. KRETCHMAR. I think you'll see why it's somewhat complicated. *(Jake looks through the photos a moment.)*

JAKE. But ... all of these photographs ...

MRS. KRETCHMAR. That's right.

JAKE. Every picture is a green hill.

MRS. KRETCHMAR. Green hills were Morgan's subject. Except for a few pictures of me, all his photos are just like those. Green hills. Thousands of them.

JAKE. Beautiful.

MRS. KRETCHMAR. He was always off somewhere, taking more pictures of more green hills. India. Asia. Australia. He died in Australia.

JAKE. *(Checks the back of a photo.)* They don't say where they were taken. There's no way to know where he took any particular picture?

MRS. KRETCHMAR. He did keep a catalogue of the hills he photographed. *(She takes out a thick account book.)* All numbered in this book.

JAKE. Great.

MRS. KRETCHMAR. The problem is, he didn't match the numbers in the book to the photographs. Alas.

JAKE. Alas. *(Mrs. Kretchmar exits as Sandy enters. Sandy and Jake speak as if on telephones.)* Sandy, it's very complicated.

SANDY. How's Finland?

JAKE. I've hardly noticed.

SANDY. It's very beautiful over here. When are you coming home?

JAKE. Well, it won't be for a while.

SANDY. Is Mrs. Kretchmar a fetching Scandinavian sex queen?

JAKE. No. Listen. I want to go through all of Kretchmar's hills.

SANDY. You can do that right here, in bed next to me.

JAKE. I mean, I want to go through his list. I want to go to all those places.

SANDY. Jake …

JAKE. I know how it sounds.

SANDY. You can't.

JAKE. I have to. I have this money I saved up.

SANDY. And then…?

JAKE. I don't know. I'll figure it out. Who knows. The first hill on the list is right here outside Helsinki. That could be the hill I'm looking for and I'll be home in no time.

SANDY. Come home, love. Please.

JAKE. I don't have time.

SANDY. What if the hill you're looking for is hill number 586, in Patagonia? Or number 2,000, in the Yukon? What if it's none of the places on that list?

JAKE. I have to take that chance. I have to stand on that hill. *(Sandy exits.)* Sandy? Sandy…? *(Loud factory noises. A Finnish worker in a hard hat enters.)*

FINNISH WORKER. *(Calling up to an unseen crane to lower something.)* O-kay! O-kay! O-kay! O-kay!

JAKE. So I go to the hill near Helsinki, and it's next to a pig iron foundry.

FINNISH WORKER. O-kay! O-kay!

JAKE. It isn't anything like the hill I'm looking for. Too flat on top, for one thing.

FINNISH WORKER. *(To Jake.)* You! Go away to hell!

JAKE. I move on down my list. South to Germany ... *(The Finnish worker exits and factory noises stop. Two German tourists enter, with binoculars.)* Hill Number 24. A very promising hill outside of Heidelberg.

FIRST GERMAN TOURIST. *Das ist ja wunderschön. ["Isn't that beautiful."]*

SECOND GERMAN TOURIST. *Wunderschön.*

JAKE. No rocks or trees. Gently rounded hilltop. The air moist and fresh, like an early morning in spring ...

FIRST GERMAN TOURIST. *Wie ein Kunstwerk! ["Like a work of art!"]*

SECOND GERMAN TOURIST. *Wie ein Kunstwerk! Genau! ["A work of art, exactly!"]*

JAKE. For a second, I think I've hit it.

FIRST GERMAN TOURIST. *Wunderschön.*

JAKE. But the grass isn't right. Not quite green enough.

FIRST GERMAN TOURIST. *Gimma? ["Go?"]*

SECOND GERMAN TOURIST. *Gimma. (German tourists exit as Sandy enters. As if on telephones.)*

SANDY. If I had you here, I could hold you in my arms and look in your eyes. If you could only look in mine ...

JAKE. Sandy, don't do this.

SANDY. My eyes are green. Remember that? I'll stand in for your green hill. No rocks or trees on me. I'll slope at the right angle for you. I'll climate-control myself to the right springlike temperature. Name it.

JAKE. I can't come back yet.

SANDY. All right.

JAKE. I can't.

SANDY. Where are you? Never mind. It doesn't matter. I don't even want to know.

JAKE. I feel like I'm getting closer. Sandy ... Hello...? *(Sandy has exited. A Britisher enters.)*

BRITISHER. We call this geological protuberance "Pigeon Hill."

JAKE. Then I have an odd experience on Hill 62, near the Scottish border.

BRITISHER. Wordsworth wrote a poem sitting here on Pigeon Hill. I don't know which poem, I'm not really as up on my Wordsworth as perhaps I should be. *(A searching woman in a shawl has entered and now moves about exploring the area around them.)*

JAKE. A woman is on the hill looking around, and there's something about her …

BRITISHER Poet laureate, you know.

JAKE. There's something so familiar about the way she's looking the place over, I wonder if she could be on the same quest I am.

BRITISHER Maybe it was Shelley, now I think of it.

JAKE. I'm sorry, would you excuse me?

BRITISHER. Oh, I beg your pardon! — Bloody Americans … *(Britisher exits.)*

JAKE. *(To Searching Woman.)* Pardon me …

SEARCHING WOMAN. *Shah-pleepto? ["Excuse me."]*

JAKE. Can I ask … what you're doing here? You? Here, doing what?

SEARCHING WOMAN. *Proo desh-ya. Nyeh por nyookto Angleeka. ["I'm sorry, I don't speak English."]*

JAKE. You. Up here. Why.

SEARCHING WOMAN. *Bloy drah-mee, eh? Bloy drah-mee. Drah-mee. ["Very beautiful."]*

JAKE. Yes. Bloy drah-mee … Are you looking for a green hill, too? This. Hill. You. Look for? Hill? Green?

SEARCHING WOMAN. *Vlop?*

JAKE. Vlop …

SEARCHING WOMAN. *Vlop?*

JAKE. Vlop … Vlop …

SEARCHING WOMAN. *Proo desh-ya … ["I'm sorry".]*

JAKE. That's okay. Thank you.

SEARCHING WOMAN. Thank you.

JAKE. Thank you. *(Searching Woman exits.)*

TELEPHONE OPERATOR'S VOICE. I will search under that spelling, sir. First name Sandra?

JAKE. Sandra, that's right. I know she's in the book.

TELEPHONE OPERATOR'S VOICE. I'm sorry, sir. It's a new number, unlisted.

JAKE. Unlisted? But …

TELEPHONE OPERATOR'S VOICE. I'm not allowed to give that number out, sir.

JAKE. All right. Thank you, operator. Thirty-three hills into Switzerland, I run out of money near the Matterhorn and take a job in a restaurant. *(Italian restaurant owner enters.)*

ITALIAN RESTAURANT OWNER. Hey, Mr. Dream-Boy! Where is tortellini verde? The peoples are waiting!

JAKE. It's coming!

ITALIAN RESTAURANT OWNER. *Subito! Subito!* Chop chop!

JAKE. Switzerland takes me two years.

ITALIAN RESTAURANT OWNER. I fire you! *Addio! (Italian restaurant owner exits.)*

JAKE. Europe takes four years altogether. Africa eats up another six. India's three. Asia takes twelve. *(Afghani enters.)*

AFGHANI. Kill that man! Kill him! KILL HIM!

JAKE. Outside Kabul, I almost get hanged by an angry mob.

AFGHANI. This man is here to take our land!

JAKE. I'm just looking for a hill (I said).

AFGHANI. He is good for nothing, and I say we must hang him on this hill until he is dead! *(Afghani exits.)*

JAKE. Hill 6973, in Tibet. Every American I meet, I ask if they know Sandy. *(American enters.)*

AMERICAN. Don't recognize the name. So what are you doing over here? Great food, huh? Talk about spicy! Don't drink the water, though. You believe the toilets here? WOW! *(American exits.)*

JAKE. I figure Sandy's long married with a family by now. She probably has a nice house with a big yard and kids running around in it. But wait. Kids? That'd be years ago. Sandy wasn't yesterday. Sandy was years and years ago. Decades. This is what I'm thinking one day in Adelaide, Australia, the day I visit the grave of Morgan Kretchmar. He isn't buried on a green hill, he's in a cemetery as flat as a starched bedsheet. And while I'm standing there over his headstone, I see a familiar face … *(Searching Woman enters. To her.)* Hello.

SEARCHING WOMAN. *Shah-pleepto?*

JAKE. You again. Me again. I guess you haven't found the hill.

SEARCHING WOMAN. *Proo desh-ya. Nyeh por nyookto Angleeka.*

JAKE. England. Pigeon Hill. You remember me?

SEARCHING WOMAN. *Proo desh-ya …*

JAKE. Suddenly I can't remember what the hill I'm looking for looks like. I close my eyes but I can't see anything anymore.

Nothing. There's no landscape behind my eyes of any kind. As if, running through the world, I've used the world up. And I'm nowhere at all, inside my head or out of it.

SEARCHING WOMAN. Thank you!

JAKE. Thank you!

SEARCHING WOMAN. Thank you!

JAKE. Thank you! *(Searching Woman exits.)* It's time to go home. *(HE puts a hand out and a Passerby drops a coin into it.)* Thank you! *(To a Second Passerby.)* Help a guy out? I'm trying to get home. *(Second Passerby drops a coin into his hand.)* Thank you, sir ... ! *(Second Passerby exits.)* I don't have a place, I'm living in a kind of a, well, it's a shelter, not a bad place. And tonight I get my passage money together. Morning comes, I gather up my pack and I'm walking out of the shelter when my foot hits a little bump, it hits the doorsill and I sort of trip ... and suddenly I feel grass under my feet. *(The Green Hill appears all around him.)*

JAKE. Very soft grass, very springy. Deep green, like pasture. The sky's a very pale blue. A few thin clouds. The air is moist and fresh, slightly cool. Like an early morning in spring. And I'm headed up the slope, angling left up the green hill. The top is right up there, I'm just about to get to it, and God, it's wonderful up here. I've never felt so free in my life. *(Sandy appears.)*

SANDY. What's on the top, up ahead of you?

JAKE. Nothing. Just the hilltop, and then sky.

SANDY. Are there any trees?

JAKE. No. No trees. No rocks or stones. Nothing.

SANDY. Birdsong? What do you hear?

JAKE. Nothing. Just the breeze.

SANDY. What's behind you, at the bottom of the hill?

JAKE. I don't know. I'm looking upwards, toward the top.

SANDY. Look back now. Turn around and look back down the hill. *(Pause.)*

JAKE. I can't. I'm looking the other way, upwards. That way. Maybe fifty more paces and I'll be on the very top.

SANDY. Am I with you?

JAKE. I don't know ...

SANDY. Look around. Do you see me?

JAKE. I can't look around.

SANDY. Am I there with you? Am I there?

JAKE. Yes. Yes. You're with me. You're here.

SANDY. Open your eyes, Jake. *(Jake opens his eyes and looks at her.)*
JAKE. You're here, you're with me.
SANDY. Welcome home. *(Sandy and the Green Hill remain. Then the Green Hill dissipates, and the lights fade.)*

End of Play

PROPERTY LIST

Poster of green hill
Portfolio with photos
Hard hat
Thick account book
Binoculars
Shawl
Coin

SOUND EFFECTS

Loud factory noises
Phone operator's voice

HAPPY

BY ALAN ZWEIBEL

HAPPY was originally produced in the Summer Shorts Festival at 59E59 in New York City. It was directed by Fred Berner. The cast was as follows:

DONALD .... Scott Adsit
HAPPY .... Arthur French

HAPPY

The vestibule of an apartment building. Nothing out of the ordinary: a door one enters from the street, a small area with a directory on the wall listing tenants, and another door for which one either has to use a key or be buzzed by a tenant to open.

Drab is the motif here. Chipped paint, faint vestiges of graffiti that defiantly still peep through the efforts of a whitewash, and lighting a few watts dimmer than it really should be. The overall feeling is that although the place is clean and well maintained, it is probably part of a low-income housing development that years and lack of funds may finally have caught up to.

The time is 1997.

At rise: Donald Rappaport (42) opens the outside door and enters the vestibule. He is wearing a suit and a Rolex watch and looks extremely hot, his forehead is beading with perspiration and the underarms of his suit jacket are drenched with huge wet spots.

He scans the directory, finds the name he's looking for, tries to open the inside door, realizes it's locked, then pushes the button next to the name on the directory.

While waiting for a response, he tries to cool off by fanning himself with his attaché case.

DONALD. Fucking hot. *(He pushes the button again and while waiting for a response tries to cool off by fanning himself with his tie.)* So fucking hot. *(He pushes the button a third time and while waiting for a response tries to cool off by fanning himself by opening and closing the outside door a number of times.)* Fucking Florida. *(Through the intercom we hear the offstage voice of an older man.)*

MAN'S VOICE. Yes?

DONALD. Mr. Haliday?

MAN'S VOICE. Who'd like to know?

DONALD. I would.

MAN'S VOICE. And you would be...?

DONALD. From New York.

MAN'S VOICE. And you think that narrows it down?

DONALD. Oh, don't mind me. I'm just a little disoriented. You see, my parents live in Boca Raton and I just flew here with my wife and kids because tonight's the first night of Passover.

MAN'S VOICE. And you think *that* narrows it down? This time of year everyone from New York comes to Florida.

DONALD. Well, I wouldn't say *everyone*.

MAN'S VOICE. Oh, that's right. The Son of Sam celebrates Passover in prison.

DONALD. Look, my name is Donald Rappaport and, after we landed in West Palm Beach, I rented a Ford Taurus and dropped everyone off at my folks' place in Boca and then drove straight here, on I-95, to Delray Beach to try to find George Haliday because I want to speak to him. Are you him?

MAN'S VOICE. I *could* be. But only on one condition.

DONALD. Which is?

MAN'S VOICE. That I don't have to hear one more word about your itinerary. Deal?

DONALD. Deal.

MAN'S VOICE. Then yes, I *am* George Haliday.

DONALD. *The* George Haliday?

MAN'S VOICE. *A* George Haliday.

DONALD. But I'm looking for *the* George Haliday.

MAN'S VOICE. *The* George Haliday who's the superintendent of this building?

DONALD. No, *the* George Haliday who used to play for the Mets.

MAN'S VOICE. Oh, *that the* George Haliday.

DONALD. Yes, *that the* George Haliday. Are you him?

MAN'S VOICE. I was.

DONALD. Well, that makes no sense.

MAN'S VOICE. How come?

DONALD. Because you're either *the* George Haliday who used to play for the Mets or you're not. It's not like you used to play for the Mets but you no longer used to play for them. You either did or you didn't, so you either are or you aren't.

MAN'S VOICE. Ow!

DONALD. Something wrong?

MAN'S VOICE. Yeah, I just threw my back out trying to follow that speech.

DONALD. You're making fun of me now ...

MAN'S VOICE. May I remind you, sir, that I am a janitor. Break it, I'll fix it. Soil it, I'll clean it. Anything more complicated, I have to call somebody. Please don't make me have to do that with this conversation.

DONALD. Okay. All I want to know is ...

MAN'S VOICE. ... if I'm the George Haliday who once played baseball.

DONALD. Yes.

MAN'S VOICE. Yes.

DONALD. You are?

MAN'S VOICE. Yes.

DONALD. You're Happy Haliday?

MAN'S VOICE. I'm Happy Haliday.

DONALD. Great!

MAN'S VOICE. Now, is there something you'd like to talk to me about?

DONALD. Yes, very much.

MAN'S VOICE. And you would like to have this talk face to face?

DONALD. Yes, I would.

MAN'S VOICE. So then I'll buzz you in, okay?

DONALD. Okay.

MAN'S VOICE. See how simple life can be if you just get to the point? *(The buzzer to the inner lobby sounds, Donald pushes it open, enters the lobby and approaches the door on the SL wall. He waits, patiently, for it to open. While he does, he fixes his hair and collar as if primping himself for an important meeting. The door opens and George "Happy" Haliday appears. He is a 64-year-old black man with gray hair, eyeglasses and an infectious smile. He walks with the aid of a cane.)* George Haliday. *(Donald just stands there, as if mesmerized.)* You okay? *(Donald's in awe.)* Will you be talking soon?

DONALD. Oh, sorry. Donald Rappaport. I guess I'm just a little starstruck. *(Happy looks around at the setting; taking in the mundane dinginess of it all.)*

HAPPY. Well, I can see how all this can be overwhelming. But don't worry. I think you'll find that we janitors are just like ordinary people — once you get past all the glitter and the goddamn paparazzi. So ... Donald ... *Que pasa?*

DONALD. I used to watch you play.

HAPPY. Oh, yeah?

DONALD. Yeah. My dad worked in the city ... I'm originally from Long Island. There's a shocker, huh?

HAPPY. Yeah, I would've bet Kenya. So, you were telling me about your dad.

DONALD. All I was saying is that lots of times I would go to work with him on the weekends, and afterwards we'd drive up to the Polo Grounds and I'd see you play. I was eight.

HAPPY. Polo Grounds ain't there no more, huh?

DONALD. The city knocked it down and put up apartment buildings a few years after the Mets moved into Shea.

HAPPY. And is that how you found out where I lived? From the Mets?

DONALD. No. I learned you were down here from that article I read about you.

HAPPY. What article?

DONALD. In the *New York Post.* That series you were in?

HAPPY. What series?

DONALD. Oh, it was no big deal ...

HAPPY. Go ahead. Tell me.

DONALD. ... *The New York Post,* in their sports section, has a feature called "What Might've Been." And, about a month ago, they had a piece ...

HAPPY. About me?

DONALD. I'm sorry. From the way it was written, I just assumed that they spoke to you ...

HAPPY. What'd they have? A lot of that next Willie Mays stuff?

DONALD. Yeah ... *(Donald follows Happy into the living room. Happy heads towards an offstage kitchen.)*

HAPPY. I'm going to get some water. How about you? Want anything?

DONALD. Yeah, I'll have a slice of apple pie, heated up, and a large milk. *(Happy peers around the kitchen wall and stares at Donald.)*

108

HAPPY. Oh, really? Now would that be regular milk or two percent?

DONALD. Make that two percent. I'm watching my weight. That way, I can have fifty glasses of two percent milk for every one glass of whole milk. *(Happy reenters the living room holding two bottles of water. He hands Donald one of them.)*

HAPPY. Here's your pie.

DONALD. On second thought, I'll just have some water.

HAPPY. Damn, and here I was so looking forward to cooking for you. So, what are we talking about? *(Donald opens his attaché case and takes out a clear plastic cube that has a baseball inside that's covered with signatures inside.)*

DONALD. Here. Check this out. *(He hands the cube to Happy.)*

HAPPY. Wow …

DONALD. The 1962 team. Pretty amazing, huh?

HAPPY. No pun intended.

DONALD. Oh. No. Although that *was* the year they started calling you guys the Amazin' Mets, right?

HAPPY. Right. Our amazing team that lost 120 games, which I believe is still the record for the most losses in one season by any Major League team in baseball history.

DONALD. Yeah, it still is.

HAPPY. Look at the names. Casey, there's Gil Hodges, Elio Chacon …

DONALD. Yeah, my grandmother got really excited when she first heard Elio Chacon's name because she thought he was Jewish. *(Happy stares at him.)* She thought it was Eliosha Cohen. *(Happy continues to stare.)* True story. *(Happy continues to stare.)* Now you're going to make fun of me?

HAPPY. No, not yet. *(Re: the ball.)* Say, is it okay if I take this out of the cube?

DONALD. Are your hands clean?

HAPPY. Excuse me? *(Donald grabs Happy's hands and examines them.)* Look, I just want to see it, not perform surgery on it.

DONALD. Yeah, I guess they're alright.

HAPPY. I'm flattered. *(Donald takes the ball out of the cube and hands it to Happy.)*

DONALD. But try to hold it by the seams.

HAPPY. Are you always so annoying?

DONALD. *(Nodding his head.)* Pretty much.

HAPPY. So, where'd you get this ball?

DONALD. My dad ... like I said, we used to go to the games all the time. He'd been a New York Giants fan, you know, before they moved to San Francisco. So when the National League came back to the city, well, it didn't matter that the Mets stunk. In fact, that was part of the charm. I'd sit there and see the players letting groundballs go through their legs, and tripping over their feet when they were rounding bases, and bumping into each other in the outfield, and I'd look at my dad and say "I can do that," and he'd look back at me and say "I believe you can," and we'd laugh about that all the way home. *(Donald laughs at the memory.)*

HAPPY. So, where'd you get this ball?

DONALD. You see, the Yankees were too good. They were exciting. But there was no way an average kid like me could ever actually relate to those guys. But you ... *(Again Donald shakes his head and savors the memory.)*

HAPPY. Ball? Get? Where?

DONALD. Well, look who's being annoying now? And where's my pie? ... I got this ball the first day you played for the Mets.

HAPPY. Really?

DONALD. They'd just brought you up. On September first. The day the teams can expand their rosters for the final pennant drive, right?

HAPPY. Yeah. There I was, sitting in some Holiday Inn in Syracuse, when they call me with the news that I'm going up — for the pennant drive to a team who was fifty-seven games out of first place with only twenty-eight left to play — and it was the greatest day of my life. They gave me a plane ticket, I called my folks, and when I landed in New York and stepped up to that plate for the first time, I was ...

DONALD. Happy.

HAPPY. Happy. I grew up across the street from the Polo Grounds. Used to watch Willie Mays do what he did from our kitchen window. So now here I am, playing his old position, hitting those two homeruns and I'm ...

DONALD. Happy.

HAPPY. Happy. And that's what I told those sportswriters and that's how that whole Happy Haliday business got started. All those banners, those pins, that billboard near the Holland Tunnel ...

DONALD. That's also when my dad started calling me that.

HAPPY. Happy?

DONALD. Uh-huh.

HAPPY. Happy Rappaport?

DONALD. Well, I'll admit it didn't have the same ring to it that Happy Haliday did, but dads don't usually say the last name when they're calling their kids, so it worked out okay ... This ball? The second time you were up?

HAPPY. The single?

DONALD. The pitch before it.

HAPPY. The foul ball?

DONALD. This is it.

HAPPY. That's the ball?

DONALD. Yep. We were sitting in the second level, behind the plate, and this ball came screaming back at us. I brought my glove to the game but there was no way I was going to catch this thing without it ripping my entire arm off my body. So my dad just nonchalantly reached over, stuck his huge meat hook of a hand in front of me, snagged the ball out of the air and said "Here you go." And here we are. It's thirty-five years later, and this is still the closest I've ever come to catching a foul ball at a game.

HAPPY. And what about those signatures? I don't remember swinging at any balls that had all those names on it.

DONALD. Those I got on the last day of that season. Someone who worked for my dad had a friend who got us passes to the clubhouse. So I brought this ball so I could get your autograph after the game. I ended up getting everybody's except yours. We waited for you but ... you never came back from the hospital. So we went home and just figured we'd get your autograph the following season.

HAPPY. Sorry. Imagine how *I* felt, though. I get hit by a pitch, run to first, steal second, steal third, score on a sacrifice fly, collapse in the dugout, taken to Lennox Hill for "precautionary" X-rays, and the next thing I know they're drilling holes in my skull because I had blood clots. Before that day, I'd never even heard of blood clots; but now I had some and they were going to keep me from doing the only thing I ever cared about doing.

DONALD. I wrote to you that winter.

HAPPY. A lot of people sent cards, get well wishes ... at one point they were actually delivering mail that was just addressed to "Happy, New York City."

DONALD. *(Joking.)* That was me.

HAPPY. *(Playing along.)* You sent those?

DONALD. Yeah. My father said you needed your rest so I just wrote "Happy, New York City" on the envelope and put a blank sheet of paper inside because I didn't want to tire you out by making you read too many words.

HAPPY. I appreciated it. Your father still call you "Happy" after it was all over for me?

DONALD. Yeah.

HAPPY. Really?

DONALD. A lot. He always pointed to you as an example of how a person should enjoy life in the moment because you never know what's waiting around the corner.

HAPPY. You mean, sort of like a "Man makes plans and God laughs" kind of thing?

DONALD. No, I'd say more along the lines of "Be careful what you wish for because you might get it."

HAPPY. ... Why?

DONALD. Because you got hit in the head with a ninety-mile-an-hour fastball.

HAPPY. I didn't wish for that.

DONALD. ... Oh, right.

HAPPY. Who would wish for a thing like that?

DONALD. I see. So maybe it was more in the "smile is a frown turned upside down" area.

HAPPY. Yeah, that must've been it. *(Donald looks at his watch.)* Late for something?

DONALD. Huh?

HAPPY. You keep looking at your watch.

DONALD. Oh, just a habit.

HAPPY. What time's your seder?

DONALD. Sundown.

HAPPY. And what time is sundown?

DONALD. Whatever time everybody's hungry. It's a Jewish thing. Look, would you mind signing that ball?

HAPPY. *(Surprised.)* You want my autograph?

DONALD. Yeah.

HAPPY. You sure? I can't remember the last time someone asked me to sign something that didn't have an invoice number on it.

DONALD. You're the only name that's missing on it and it would mean a lot.

HAPPY. If you say so. *(Donald reaches into his jacket pocket, pulls out a fancy pen and hands it to Happy.)* How should I do this?

DONALD. Well, you just find an open spot on the ball and sign your name there.

HAPPY. I mean the pen. Where's the point on this thing?

DONALD. Oh. *(Showing him.)* You just twist the top and … there you go.

HAPPY. And what about this shit over here?

DONALD. What shit?

HAPPY. This rubber shit. *(Happy shows him the pen.)*

DONALD. Oh, that's just a padding to rest your fingers on while you're writing. *(Happy stares at him.)* It's really comfortable. *(Happy continues to stare.)* It was a gift. *(Happy continues to stare.)* You're going to make fun of me now?

HAPPY. *(Nodding.)* You've given me no choice.

DONALD. Go ahead.

HAPPY. Ready?

DONALD. *(Bracing himself.)* Yes.

HAPPY. You're a Sissy Mary.

DONALD. … That's it?

HAPPY. That's it.

DONALD. Well, you nailed my fat ass on that one. So, now that that's over with … *(Indicating ball.)* if you don't mind.

HAPPY. Boy, I'm really honored. *(He spins the ball in his hand, looking for a place to sign.)*

DONALD. There's a spot.

HAPPY. Where?

DONALD. Between Marv Throneberry and Choo Choo Coleman.

HAPPY. Little tight, don't you think?

DONALD. Not really …

HAPPY. Oh, here we go. Now should it be "To Donald" or "Don" or one of your kids…?

DONALD. No, no, no. Just your name.

HAPPY. But …

DONALD. It shouldn't be "To" anyone.

HAPPY. But you flew down, you landed in West Palm Beach, you drove the rented Taurus to my house. I feel like I should say something special.

DONALD. I appreciate that but it's much more valuable if it's not personalized to anyone.

HAPPY. What do you mean by more valuable?

DONALD. It's worth more.

HAPPY. To who?

DONALD. To a buyer.

HAPPY. Excuse me?

DONALD. Well, if a collector is in the market for something like this, he's more apt to pay top dollar if it just has the athlete's name on it — as opposed to something that's made out to a specific person, because when he goes to sell it, *his* buyer might not want a ball that's made out to someone else.

HAPPY. *(Suspicious.)* You know, we both know what I do for a living, but I don't believe we ever got around to talking about what you do, Mr. Rappaport?

DONALD. I deal sports memorabilia. *(He hands Happy a business card.)*

HAPPY. *(Reading.)* "The Sports Kingdom."

DONALD. I have four stores in the tri-state area.

HAPPY. So let me see if I understand this correctly. This ball with all these autographs on it, is worth money.

DONALD. Yes.

HAPPY. And if I write my autograph on it …

DONALD. It will be worth more money.

HAPPY. Why?

DONALD. There'd be no other ball like it. That original team. Three of them Hall of Famers — based on the careers they had with other teams before they came to the Mets, mind you. But still, they're dead, so they can never sign another ball ever again and the rest of these players are probably scattered all over the country and it would take a fortune to go track them down.

HAPPY. So how much could you get?

DONALD. For that ball?

HAPPY. Approximately.

DONALD. I can tell you exactly.

HAPPY. So tell me exactly.

DONALD. Twenty-thousand.

HAPPY. Dollars?

DONALD. That's right.

HAPPY. So let me see if I understand this correctly. You actually think that you can take this ball and sell it for exactly …

DONALD. I *know* I can sell that ball for exactly $28,000.

HAPPY. And how's that?

DONALD. It's already sold.

HAPPY. It is?

DONALD. Yes. Once you sign it, that is.

HAPPY. And, just so I know, how did that happen?

DONALD. I know a man up in New Jersey whose name is Joe Eastern, and he's a collector and he called me. You see Happy, there's so much memorabilia out there, the market is so flooded, that many collectors like to specialize in just one particular category that they have a passion for. The 1961 Yankees is a big attraction. Anything to do with Muhammad Ali, some of the great Boston Celtic teams, you know … and this guy …

HAPPY. Joe Eastern.

DONALD. That's right. Joe Eastern …

HAPPY. He the one who gave you this Sissy Mary pen as a gift?

DONALD. No, but he did tell me that he grew up on Long Island and that he was eleven years old when the Mets came into existence and I told him I had a game used ball with the original team's signatures on it with the exception of yours and he said if you signed it, well, I negotiated a price of $28,000.

HAPPY. So you're going to part with this ball.

DONALD. Yes.

HAPPY. This ball that's filled with all those happy memories of when your hero dad caught it.

DONALD. Well, yeah …

HAPPY. *(Raising his voice.)* That same dad who called you Happy. After me, by the way. Who the hell are you, Mr. Rappaport? I played baseball because I loved it. I still love it. Every year I stop by those spring training camps when the teams are down here — they don't know me from a hole in the ground. To them I'm just another fan and they're right. I am a fan. And you told me that you were one, too. But now I see that all you really came here was to get an old man's signature on this ball so you can peddle memories for a profit.

DONALD. Happy …

HAPPY. No, Mr. Rappaport! You're not a fan!

DONALD. Happy …

HAPPY. You're a scavenger!

DONALD. Happy!

HAPPY. A parasite who feeds off those who actually add something to the world!

115

DONALD. Happy!

HAPPY. What!

DONALD. I came here *to* give you this ball.

HAPPY. ... Excuse me? Would you mind indulging an old man by repeating that last sentence one more time? Just in case I die?

DONALD. Joe Eastern offered me $25,000 for the ball. But I insisted on exactly twenty-eight thousand — which is exactly $1,000 for every game you played in the major leagues. It's not a lot by today's standards but I just thought there was a certain ring to the way it sounded.

HAPPY. So let me see if I understand this correctly. I sign this ball ...

DONALD. And Joe Eastern owes you $28,000.

HAPPY. I just shamed you into this, didn't I?

DONALD. No ...

HAPPY. Me calling you a scavenger and a parasite and a bottom feeder ...

DONALD. You didn't call me a bottom feeder ...

HAPPY. That's because you interrupted me. I was on the verge of calling you that and a lot worse.

DONALD. Oh. Sorry I interrupted. I would've loved to have heard you top Sissy Mary.

HAPPY. So right from the time you buzzed my button you were going to do this?

DONALD. Yeah.

HAPPY. No. Something's wrong with this story.

DONALD. Why do you say that?

HAPPY. It doesn't add up.

DONALD. What doesn't add up? Happy ...

HAPPY. You know, I've tried my best all these years not to be bitter. That doesn't do anyone any good. One newspaper guy once figured out that if I'd kept up those numbers I had, you know, over the length of a normal career, I'd be in the Hall of Fame. Well, that kind of talk don't do anyone any good either. Sure, it would have been great if I was Happy Haliday for longer than I was. But I wasn't. So I try my best not to mourn for the life I didn't have. And I think I'm doing an okay job. We raised five kids in this place, my wife and I. She worked, I worked and somehow we managed to send five happy people out into this world. But now you come here offering me this incredible generosity — Jesus, more money than I've ever seen in any one place at any one time, and one part of me wants to cry and another part is suspicious and says that this doesn't add up. That there's a lie here that hasn't been said yet.

DONALD. There's no lie, Happy. Here. Here's Joe Eastern's phone number. Call him and see for yourself that ...

HAPPY. No, no. I believe that part.

DONALD. Then what part don't you believe? The Taurus? I swear to you I rented a Ford Taurus. I'm not proud of it. But look outside, it's right by the curb.

HAPPY. *(Shaking his head.)* It's the pacing. The constant looking at your watch, I've seen executive types before. Suits, tiny phones that make them look like they're talking into their hands. Guys who are here but on their way to there. Are there but have to cut it short because they're already late somewhere else. Basically we're talking about guys who are never where they want to be. So now I look at you and do my best to figure out where you're supposed to be instead of here. Can you tell me that? Where you *really* should be right now.

DONALD. In Boca.

HAPPY. With your family.

DONALD. Yeah.

HAPPY. But instead you came down here. You read an article, flew down, and drove a rented Taurus to Delray beach so you can give someone you never met a $28,000 baseball an hour before the start of a holiday dinner when you're going to be here in Florida for how long?

DONALD. Seven days.

HAPPY. But Passover lasts eight days.

DONALD. Yeah, but the shiva lasts seven.

HAPPY. The shiva?

DONALD. The mourning period. My father died last night. We flew down here for his funeral.

HAPPY. *(Sympathetic.)* There's more, right?

DONALD. *(Nodding.)* We hadn't spoken in years. We had a fight and I got real pissed at him, and he got real pissed at me, and we were both acting like we were going to live forever and had all the time in the world to make up with each other.

HAPPY. What was the fight about?

DONALD. We both forgot. But we were both stubborn. My Mom tried to intervene. My sisters, my brother ... All I know is that I was starting to miss him and then, about a month ago, that

117

article about you was in the *New York Post* and I sent it to my dad with a note attached to it that said, "Remember?" And a few days later I got a package in the mail. A box. Inside of it was this ball, and a note which said, "Yes, I remember." I called him and we stayed on the phone for over three hours and at the end of the conversation decided that we would give you this ball together — when I came down for Passover. Then around 3:00 this morning my mom phoned. He had a heart attack.

HAPPY. Had you two spoken since that three-hour call?

DONALD. *(Smiling.)* Every night.

HAPPY. *(Smiling.)* No shit?

DONALD. *(Smiling.)* No shit.

HAPPY. So I did good?

DONALD. You did real good. Thanks. *(A beat. Donald checks his watch, and then:)* Look, I should be getting back to my parents' house. Here's Joe Eastern's number. After you sign the ball, why not give him a buzz and you can work out all the details with him directly.

HAPPY. Well, I'm not sure I want to do that.

DONALD. Oh, would you like me to call him for you?

HAPPY. No. I'm just not so sure that I want to sell this thing so fast.

DONALD. Happy ...

HAPPY. I know, I know — there's a lot anyone can do with $28,000. But just like you have your quirky ways about you, I was brought up to feel that a man should not accept any gift that he himself could not afford to have given.

DONALD. Don't let false pride enter this, Happy. Because I don't know exactly how much it was worth your getting me and my Dad back together again but, as far as I'm concerned, I'm the one who got the bargain. But the decision is yours. There's the ball. And there's the phone number ... Take care, Happy Haliday.

HAPPY. You too, Happy Rappaport. *(Donald picks up his attaché case and turns to leave.)*

DONALD. Bye.

HAPPY. Hey, Donald?

DONALD. Yeah?

HAPPY. Thank you.

DONALD. Sure. *(Donald exits the apartment, crosses the lobby and opens the door to the vestibule.)*

HAPPY. *(Thru intercom.)* And, Donald?

DONALD. Yeah?

HAPPY. *(Thru intercom.)* Next Passover? If you and your family should decide to fly down to Flordia?

DONALD. Yeah?

HAPPY. *(Thru intercom.)* I'd really love it if you had the seder here, in my apartment.

DONALD. Really?

HAPPY. *(Thru intercom.)* Yeah. That way I could get to cook that big meal for you we were talking about earlier.

DONALD. And pie?

HAPPY. *(Thru intercom.)* Yes, pie. *(Lights start to fade.)*

DONALD. A la mode?

HAPPY. *(Thru intercom.)* Don't push it. *(Donald exits the building. Lights fade out.)*

End of Play

PROPERTY LIST

Rolex watch
Attaché case with clear cube and baseball inside
Glasses
Cane
Two bottles water
Fancy pen
Business card

SOUND EFFECTS

Buzzer
Intercom voice of old man

A SECOND OF PLEASURE

BY NEIL LaBUTE

A SECOND OF PLEASURE was first produced by ThroughLine Artists (J.J. Kandel and John McCormack, Producing Directors) as part of Summer Shorts 3 at 59E59 Theaters in New York City in 2009. It was directed by Andrew McCarthy. The cast was as follows:

JESS .... Margaret Colin
KURT .... Victor Slezak

A SECOND OF PLEASURE

Silence. Darkness.

Two people standing at Grand Central. Near the clock.

Let's call them "Kurt" and "Jess." He is studying the train tick-et in his hand. She waits patiently for him. Looks at her watch. Each of them carries a travel bag.

After a moment, she stops. Looks at him. Speaks.

JESS. ... Alright, here's the thing.
KURT. What?
JESS. The thing of it is, I don't really want to go. I don't. I guess that would be the actual "thing" of it.
KURT. Oh.
JESS. Yeah.
KURT. I see.
JESS. I know I'm standing here and I've got my bag in my hand and all that, but if you were to ask me right now, "Hey, you sure you wanna do this, go up to the country this weekend?" I'd say, "No, not really." I would, I'd say that. "No thank you, I don't." *(Kurt nods at this, looking around the place. Busy people moving past the two of them. Checks his watch.)*
KURT. But ... you already said yes before.
JESS. I know I did.
KURT. I mean before now. Today. This minute. You said yes earlier this week.
JESS. You're right. I did do that.
KURT. And that was, like, Tuesday or something.
JESS. Late Tuesday, I think, but yeah. Yes, it was.

KURT. So, I mean … you had all week to say something. *(Beat.)* Train boards in, like, ten minutes…

JESS. I realize this is sudden. Unexpected.

KURT. Very. It's very much that…

JESS. I know. I didn't want to do this. I mean, I did, I did want to tell you earlier … call you or something, an email … but then today I had this … a thing happen. Something happened, and it gave me this idea that I should say something.

KURT. So … you gave it a lot of thought, then?

JESS. Huh?

KURT. I mean, it didn't just pop into your head this minute, when we were buying tickets or whatever. You mulled it over.

JESS. Well, I didn't … you know, I wasn't up at night because of it, but yeah. I tried to find the right approach to … but then I'm suddenly standing there buying snacks and thinking to myself, "Gosh, I really need to say something! I do, and right now."

KURT. Oh. *(Silence as Kurt tries to think of something to say — a proper comeback or the like. Jess jumps in to help.)*

JESS. That's what I was doing when you touched my shoulder and said, "You okay?" That's what I was doing at that very moment.

KURT. I see.

JESS. I was coming to a decision about it.

KURT. Without me.

JESS. No! I mean, yes, alright — it's not like I was purposefully trying to leave you out, it's just that, you know, it's sort of a one-sided deal, that's all. Right?

KURT. I wouldn't know.

JESS. Come on…

KURT. Seriously. I'm big on sharing. On being open about stuff, whether it's painful stuff or not.

JESS. Oh, please.

KURT. I am. I'm completely that way.

JESS. Fine, I understand.

KURT. No, I don't think you do — you don't or you wouldn't approach my feelings in so cavalier a manner.

JESS. I'm not being … that's a little dramatic, isn't it?

KURT. I think it's a pretty suitable metaphor. *(She smiles and shakes her head; he holds up his hands as if to say "What do you mean?" Rolls his eyes.)*

JESS. Well, it's a bit much, I think. Plus, you couldn't really … I mean, I'm a woman. It doesn't even work, your analogy.

KURT. I know that, I do, but you get my point.

JESS. I do, yes, but it's ... it just seems kind of grand, that's all. I mean, "Cavalier?" Really?

KURT. Women can be "cavalier," too, you know. It's not just a, a, a male thing ...

JESS. No, I know, but I mean "traditionally." Traditionally it was for men. Doing ... that. Being all that way. With swords.

KURT. True, no, you're probably right. *(Beat.)* I was hurt, so I lashed out. Sorry ... *(People are having to walk around them now so Kurt signals for Jess to move aside. Near the newspaper machines.)*

JESS. I understand, I'm just saying — isn't it better that I bring this up now than in the middle of dinner tonight or tomorrow during a second set of tennis? I'm trying to be fair to both of us ...

KURT. I see. This is you being "fair."

JESS. Well, in a way, yes. Trying to be.

KURT. Great.

JESS. I really am ...

KURT. Terrific.

JESS. See, now you're just angry. Getting all huffy and everything ...

KURT. No, I'm not. I'm really not.

JESS. Sounds like it to me.

KURT. I'm not. I'm just taking it all in. Dealing with it — as our train's leaving.

JESS. It's not going yet, we've still got a few minutes.

KURT. Whatever. Doesn't really matter now, does it? It's moot.

JESS. Is it?

KURT. I think so. I think it was invented for a moment like this, that word. "Moot." Just like this moment right here ...

JESS. I don't know. What I'm saying is there's still time, whether we both go or just you — there's still time to get on board.

KURT. That's comforting...

JESS. God ... *(Beat.)* Lemme walk you down. okay? *(Kurt doesn't say anything, just turns and begins to move off. He stops, though, and looks back at her.)*

KURT. This is unbelievable.

JESS. ... I can't help it. I needed to say what I was feeling.

KURT. And you did.

JESS. Yes I did, I did do that and I'm glad. I'm sorry if it feels ... but I am glad. So. *(Beat.)* The rest is up to you ...

KURT. Wow, you've got an answer for everything today! That's great ... *(He checks his watch. She stands still and follows him with her eyes.)*

JESS. I'm just being practical. No reason that you shouldn't enjoy this — I'm just letting you know up front that I can't do it this time.

KURT. Well, not exactly "up front." No, that would've been Tuesday night, up front. Wednesday morning at the latest...

JESS. Right, yes, that's true ...

KURT. No, I think you'd have to go ahead and call this "last-minute," what you're doing here — besides thoughtless and shitty and maybe even mean-spirited. I think this would go down as "last-minute."

JESS. I deserve that, so go ahead ...

KURT. I don't know if you deserve it or not. It's just how it makes me feel ... *(He looks off into the crowd. Waits. Turns back to her.)* ... you haven't said "why" you're ... you know ... nothing about that. Yet.

JESS. Because. I feel bad for him.

KURT. Oh.

JESS. That's why. okay?

KURT. You feel "bad."

JESS. Yes, I do.

KURT. For him? You mean *him* him?

JESS. Yes. My husband.

KURT. Got it.

JESS. I was packing when it started. Going up and down stairs and throwing a suitcase together, having already laid the ground work — heading off to the Cape with some friends, getaway with the girls, blah blah blah — and I see him, sitting in the kitchen in his suit, still in his suit jacket and having cereal for dinner ... *(Beat.)* It was a kid's cereal and I was watching him, leaning forward with his tie hanging in the bowl, almost touching the milk, and it hit me. It did. Right then it kind of hit me like a shock or something, a little bolt of lightning. I sat down on the stairs and, and I ... I couldn't breathe for a minute, watching him. *(Beat.)* And I realized that I was feeling something that I hadn't felt in a long time. For him. My husband ...

KURT. My. My oh my.

JESS. Yeah, I know...

KURT. This is a surprise...

JESS. Believe me, for me, too.

126

KURT. I'm sure.

JESS. I mean, we've done this before. You know? Done it and I didn't think twice about it or what it meant or how he might feel. No, I just did it. But not today. *(Jess doesn't have anything more to offer up to Kurt than this. He just nods his head and keeps quiet for now. Finally he turns back to her. Trying to be nice.)*

KURT. ... So you can't go. That's what you're saying. Don't want to now.

JESS. No, I can't. Not this week, anyway.

KURT. Not ever, maybe, from what I'm hearing.

JESS. I'm not sure. Honestly, I don't really ... I'm confused by it myself.

KURT. Right.

JESS. I am — I hope you believe me, but this is the best I can do. Try and identify my feelings ... put my finger on it.

KURT. And I appreciate that. Would've been nice if you could've put your finger on it, like, say, Thursday or something, but ... *(Beat.)* Hotel's booked now and everything.

JESS. I know! I can pay you half of it, if that helps at all, or ...

KURT. No, come on, you know it's not just about that. The cost. Please.

JESS. I know. *(Beat.)* It was just that image of him, sitting there in the breakfast nook with that carton of Count Chocula. I saw him with a puddle of brown milk in his ... there in his bowl and it all made sense to me, what I'd been doing to him. The hurt that was piling up because of this. Us.

KURT. "Us." You mean "us" us?

JESS. Yes. You and me. *(Beat.)* But as I sat and watched him eat, trying to scoop up those little marshmallow pieces with his spoon, I felt a kind of pleasure. Only a second, really, but it was so deep and so honest that I remembered everything about why we had come together and married and had our children and lasted this long.

KURT. Jesus, that's ...

JESS. Through sickness and money troubles and recessions and a war and even you and me. We had weathered all of that and we were still together — that man in there and me. Because of a kind of pleasure we brought to each other, something that — if I'm at all honest about it — we'll probably never have a chance of finding. Us two. *(Kurt nods at her and lets out a deep breath of air. Sound of trains in the distance.)* Just being honest.

127

KURT. Yes. Brutally honest.

JESS. I'm sorry.

KURT. You could've ... I mean, you could just say "I can't make it this time." Don't have to be all Bram Stoker about it — drive a stake through my heart.

JESS. I don't know. Maybe I do.

KURT. God, that's ... shit. Wow. *(Kurt takes all this in — Jess has done nothing but tell the truth. He starts to say something but stops himself. She waits. Listening. Finally Kurt speaks. Quietly.)* ... Listen, if that's the case, then okay. I understand. Hell, I feel the same way ... every time I look at one of my kids and I say how bad I feel about missing a soccer game, that kind of thing — I don't, can't stand that crap. I hate soccer, actually — but I detest lying to them.

JESS. No, I agree. I've always hated that part of this ...

KURT. Not so much with my wife because, well, I dunno, I'm not sure. She's an adult and I'm just so used to it, after doing it so often over so many years, that it's really become not just natural but kind of, umm, comforting ... in a way. It warms me a bit, to look into her eyes and deceive her.

JESS. Oh. Well, I hope that's not true ... *(Jess studies him but can't read the guy. Good luck. After that, she turns and looks over at the tracks across the way. Finally she looks back over at Kurt — he stares at her.)*

KURT. That sounds bad. I don't mean that I'm looking for opportunities to do it, of course not. It's just that it's become a kind of ritual between us, even if she's not really in on it. It's some form of ... closeness, actually. I mean, I wouldn't lie to just anybody! I guess that's what I'm saying.

JESS. I think I understand.

KURT. *(Nodding in agreement)* ... Good. *(Beat.)* Well, I should probably get over there, then.

JESS. Alright. *(Beat.)* So you're still ... I mean, you're gonna go ahead and...?

KURT. Yeah. I mean, I already did all the legwork here, might as well try to enjoy it. I can probably get a little work done ... maybe a round of golf or something ... *(Beat.)* Or maybe even come back early, take the kids to a movie. Who knows?

JESS. That'd be nice. Weather's supposed to hold through Wednesday.

KURT. That's good.

JESS. I hope the hotel's nice. It sounds nice.

KURT. Yeah, should be. I'll cancel all of your treatments — at the spa there.

JESS. You sure? I can call if you…

KURT. No, no problem. I'll take care of it.

JESS. Fine, then. So, I guess I'll see you … *(Kurt nods as he shoulders his bag again. Speaks again.)*

KURT. When?

JESS. Ohh … I don't know, actually. I just said that. It's one of those things you say if you're not sure what else to say. Filler.

KURT. Right.

JESS. I don't know if we will. Or should, even. Not for a while.

KURT. I figured as much.

JESS. Yes. I mean, with the way I'm feeling now … it's …

KURT. Uh-huh.

JESS. We should probably — *(An overhead announcement from the ticket desk. They both look over to see passengers starting to form lines.)* I think they just called for … they're …

KURT. Yeah, I better get over there.

JESS. *(Pointing.)* Track 23.

KURT. Yep, that's it. Okay, so …

JESS. Take care.

KURT. … You too, I guess. *(They hug and then hesitate — both suddenly nervous about their surroundings rather than connected and passionate. Peck on the cheek just about does it. Kurt nods and looks at her, kindly but concerned. Touches her on the shoulder.)* … Hey listen … I was just … lemme ask you something, quick, and be honest … it seems like it's time for that. Right now. Honesty.

JESS. Alright. If I can.

KURT. Did you … in all these months together, did you ever feel that type of thing for me? *(Beat.)* What you described about the cereal and your husband with his tie in the milk there? Did you? *(He stands there, still one hand on her shoulder. Waiting for something more from her. A sign.)*

JESS. Well …

KURT. I'm not saying that exact same kind of "pleasure," but something. Anything. Did you? From what I ever did, or, or …

JESS. … Ummmmm …

KURT. … From us together? *(Beat.)* You can tell me. It's okay, I'm curious, that's all.

JESS. It's not really a fair …

KURT. Even once. Just one time. *(Beat.)* Once?

JESS. No. I didn't. No. Not ever.

KURT. Oh. Okay. Alright, I was just wondering …

JESS. I'm sorry.

KURT. No problem. It's … so, I'll see you, then.

JESS. Yeah, fine. Sometime. *(He nods and walks away. Only gets a few steps and turns.)*

KURT. Sometime soon?

JESS. Maybe. Hope so.

KURT. Be nice if it was soon.

JESS. I know.

KURT. I'm just saying, my opinion — that'd be nice. 'Soon.'

JESS. We'll see. *(Smiles.)* Have a great weekend!

KURT. Will do. *(Beat.)* Okay, see what happens …

JESS. Sounds good. *(Beat.)* I just can't promise — listen, we bump into each other all the time. Not just us but people, all of us, back and forth across the world and sometimes it's all life-and-death and other days we barely even notice. That's what we do. We pass each other, and maybe next time I'll cling to you, never let you go or, or, or maybe we'll act like we never even met. Why don't we just wait and see, okay? Life's funny that way … you know? *(Kurt reacts to this — he nods as he lets this sink in.)*

KURT. Yep. So, I'll call ya when I get … or …

JESS. No, don't do that. Don't call.

KURT. You're right. Fine. I'll just, ummm …

JESS. Okay then.

KURT. Okay.

JESS. Goodbye. *(This time she is the first to go — she nods and then turns away. Moving off toward an exit without looking back.)*

KURT. *(To himself.)* … Bye. *(Kurt remains where he is. Watching her slowly disappear into the crowd. He doesn't move. Silence. Darkness.)*

End of Play

PROPERTY LIST

Train tickets
Watch
2 travel bags

SOUND EFFECTS

Trains in distance
Overhead announcement

AN UPSET

BY DAVID AUBURN

AN UPSET was originally produced by Ensemble Studio Theatre in New York City on May 12, 2008. It was directed by Harris Yulin. The cast was as follows:

MALE 1 .... Matt Lauria
MALE 2 .... Darren Goldstein

AN UPSET

A locker room.

1 is a tennis player in his early 20s.

2 is a tennis player in his early 30s.

Several months separate each of the 3 scenes.

ONE

2 changing, furious. 1 enters.

1. Good match.
2. Fuck you.
1. I just want to say ... is an honor to be on court with you.
2. "Is an honor." Can you fucking speak English?
1. I only learn English last year. I see you are not very happy right now. I leave you alone.
2. Well thank you very much. *(Beat.)* It's just ... you fucking *qualifiers.*
1. Excuse me?
2. You play in your little qualifying tournament. You beat a bunch of granddads, and juniors on Ritalin, and country club teaching pros diddling around on the circuit for a lark, for the groupies, they're *amateurs.* But congratulations, cheers, you *won* it ... So you come into the main draw all nice and warm, feeling confident, your pecker's *up* ... meanwhile I come in after a week and a half in *New Haven* busting my ass against *top ten players,* vicious... Plus I'm ME ... I've got to walk out on that stadium court with everyone praying I'll lose. "Let's see something *new.*" "Let's see what the Czech kid can do" —

1. I am Romanian.
2. Romania. You actually have tennis courts there?

   Christ, the crowd. They're bored. They're so bored, they're jaded, they'd root for anything as long as it was "different." They're like Romans in the Coliseum: they'd root for a *giraffe* against me, or a pair of *dwarves* — of course they get on your side. You're the "underdog." "This crowd in New York sure loves an underdog." I watch the tape tonight — I gave you a nickel every time the TV guys say that, you'd walk away with ninety-five bucks. Of course, the first bad call they're on your side.

1. The ball was in.
2. *(Explodes.)* It was *not* in! It was out by a country mile! You couldn't possibly have seen it! You were sprawled on your ass twenty-five feet away! I was standing right next to it!
1. It was called in. I'm sorry you do not like it.
2. You're goddamn right I do not like it. A bad call at break point in the third and you're fucked. You're fucked.
1. Excuse me. You are not fucked.
2. Excuse *me* —
1. I had still to win three sets.
2. Have you ever heard of *momentum?* It's *all about* momentum! I go down a break in the third, and the crowd goes all giddy cause they think they're "seeing something." An Upset! An Upset "in the making"! And suddenly they're screaming your name every time you knock in a bloopy forehand — a passing shot I could make in my sleep when I was 15 brings down the house — guys in the stands, "hard-core" fans who think they're seeing something "new," being "mavericks" because they spin on a dime and start worshiping a "new face" — God, I can see the two-faced fuckers with their white shorts and their visors — why the *fuck* do tennis fans wear fucking tennis *clothes* when they go to *watch* a fucking tennis *match?* You don't see Giants fans at the fucking Meadowlands in shoulder pads, for fuck's sake. I just know those assholes were calling their asshole friends on their cell phones, saying, "Yeah, I'm in the stadium! Where are you? The food court? Hey, you gotta come over! Yeah, put down your fifteen-dollar roasted-vegetable-and-hummus wrap and come see this, I'm watching an *upset!*" All because you make a little diving volley at the net on break point that goes *out,* but everyone is too dazzled by the Romanian no-name qualifier doing his little flouncy gymnastics routine on a shot

that you could have made *vertically* like a normal man if you'd *moved your silly fucking feet* — and there goes the set. And the next two sets. And the match goes down the fucking toilet.

1. I suppose you did not lose them.

2. Oh, I lost them all right. And don't think I can't stomach it. I've lost matches before. I've even lost matches on cocksucking calls before. The thing is, what I've never done is lost a *first-round match in a major* on a cocksucking call to a 19-year-old *Romanian qualifier* ranked 164 *in the world* with a *backhand* like a postmenopausal mom playing Sunday *doubles* in the *park* with the *girls from the book group. (Beat.)*

1. You know my ranking.

2. What?

1. I did not think a man like you would know my ranking. Or my age.

2. Don't get all misty. I do my homework. What do you think?

1. My backhand is not strong, I realize this.

2. You're not turning your shoulder.

1. I am working on this.

2. You ought to be looking over your shoulder at the ball.

1. This is what my coach says.

2. You should listen to him.

1. I do. But he's in Romania.

2. Your coach didn't see your big U.S. upset because he's in Romania?

1. Yes. He is … very sick. *(Beat.)*

2. Well that's a real heartbreaker. Congratulations. The press will gobble that.

1. I think he will die soon.

2. What a shame. *(Beat.)*

1. You play him once.

2. I did?

1. Oh, yes. A great match.

2. Remind me.

1. The 1994 Australian Open. The Fourth Round.

2. Fourth Round, '94, Australia … Not the bow-legged lefty with the metal racquet.

1. He used metal racquet.

2. That was *freakish.* The last guy on the tour playing with metal! This hilarious aluminum Eastern Bloc piece of crap! It was — Yeah, yeah.

1. Yes, metal.

2. *(Remembers.)* And I got a cocksucking call *then!* You miserable Romanians! He was up a break in the fourth when I doubled at 30 – 40 on a *foot fault!* They call a foot fault *randomly* once a tournament just to show they remember the fucking rules and I got it, so this rubber-legged Romanian metal-wielding *freak* ranked seventy-fifth in the world took a second set off me!

1. He often talks of it.

2. I won the fifth, though, 7 – 5.

1. He talks of it as the great match of his life. He has picture of you and he together at the net shaking hands after the match. He keeps it above the, how do you say, the fire-piece?

2. The mantelpiece.

1. The mantelpiece. In the main room, the living room of his apartment.

2. Or you could say "fireplace." Same thing. *(Beat.)*

1. The racquet from the match is there, too. He never used it again. It's up on the wall next to the picture in a frame.

2. Well, that's where it belongs. *(Beat. 1 is finished dressing. He picks up his bag to go.)* So what's he got?

1. Cancer.

2. Too bad.

1. I should call him now. *(1 goes to exit.)*

2. Hey. *(1 turns.)* Tell him fuck you from me. *(Blackout.)*

TWO

1 dressing after a match. 2 enters, dressed in street clothes.

2. Very nice.

1. Thank you.

2. I watched the last set from the stands.

1. I saw you.

2. What is that now. Twenty-three straight? Twenty-four?

1. Twenty-one.

2. It gets so you can't remember losing?

1. I remember a little bit.
2. But it stops feeling like it can happen to you.
1. It can always happen to you.
2. Is it going to happen to you tomorrow?
1. I don't believe so. No.
2. You see? That's when you got to be careful.
1. The man tomorrow is unseeded.
2. You were unseeded a few tournaments ago. Now look at you.
1. A few tournaments from now he will be still. You can see it. In his shoulders. *(Beat.)*
2. You managed to tart up your backhand a little.
1. Yes. Is much better. Thank you for the advice.
2. Don't give me any credit for it, please. It's no longer an embarrassment, now it's merely pitiable.
1. It feels much better. Like everything.
2. Here. *(He tosses 1 a tennis ball.)*
1. What?
2. Sign it?
1. You're joking.
2. No. I would like your autograph, please.
1. I don't understand this joke.
2. It's not a joke, sadly. It's for my sister's kid. He made me promise. Evidently he's a fan.
1. You did not tell him to "fuck off"?
2. He's eleven.
1. The way you say all the time to everybody, "Fuck off, fuck you, fucking fuck"?
2. I'm not saying that wasn't the initial impulse. For a second there. Then I took a deep breath and choked down my pride, in the name of benevolent uncle-hood and for the good of the game. Need a pen?
1. No. What is his name?
2. Nate. *(1 takes out a Sharpie and signs. He tosses the ball back.)* Thank you.
1. I never want to disappoint a fan.
2. Attaboy. You're getting a lot of new fans.
1. Yes.
2. How are the girls treating you?
1. I have a girlfriend.
2. She on tour with you?
1. No.

2. Ah. Back in the old country.

1. In Bucharest, yes. She is studying.

2. A scholar.

1. Sports medicine.

2. Ah.

1. It is a very demanding course.

2. Sure, sure.

1. She works very hard.

2. Couldn't cut it as a player, figured she could stay close to you taping your knee and giving you backrubs.

1. We ... haven't decided if she will tour with me.

2. Pretty girl?

1. I think she is very pretty, yes.

2. Good. So how many have you fucked on the tour? Yours is back in Romania, you can't tell me you haven't made a few selections from the buffet outside the players' lounge. Come on, I can see it in your shoulders.

1. You are wrong.

2. Come off it. There are too many of them. The lovely spoiled little slags from all across the globe. You double up yet?

1. I'm sorry?

2. Two at once. Or three? Better do it while you can, it gets much harder after you fall out of the top 50. Come on. You can tell me. *(Beat.)*

1. Yes, I do this.

2. Attaboy. And?

1. I'm afraid I disappoint them.

2. Oh, they don't care. Get that straight in your mind and you'll be okay. They don't care about you. Once, this girl knocked on my hotel room door — I was getting ready to go to the airport — and she says, "Can I come in?" I was number three in the world. I said, "I've got to leave in 15 minutes." She says — are you ready? She says, "That's okay, I only need ten." They don't care. It's a notch on their belt, or, today, an entry in their, what is it, blog or something. You can have fun with it. Once, at a party, this girl comes right up to me — no preliminaries, no name, nothing, says, "Come into the bathroom, I want to suck your cock."

1. What did you do?

2. I said, "What's in it for me?"

1. *(Laughs.)* What did she say?

140

2. She loved it. She laughed.

1. Then she suck your cock.

2. Right. Don't worry. You didn't disappoint them. Maybe *you* were disappointed. Were you disappointed?

1. A little.

2. Yeah, I felt the same way. I'd rather be inadequate with one woman at a time.

1. I was not "inadequate."

2. Oh no, no. But it's nicer with your girlfriend.

1. Yes.

2. That's sweet. You'll try it again, though.

1. Yes.

2. That's the spirit. Keep at it. Keep trying.

1. *(Shrugs.)* I am an athlete. *(Beat.)* Can I ask you something? Something … personal?

2. Sure.

1. Who is your art dealer?

2. Uh, I don't have just one, there are a couple of guys I've worked with over the — Why?

1. I'm thinking of buying a painting.

2. Yeah? What?

1. I don't know yet. But I like always this idea of buying art. And now one day I know I'll buy a house and I will need art to put up on the walls.

2. One day? Buy a house now, the year you're having.

1. I'm not ready yet. I don't know where it should be. Florida? Spain? Monte Carlo, for the taxes?

2. Bucharest?

1. Not Bucharest. Have you been to Bucharest?

2. In and out.

1. This is the way to go. So, I read how you are famous for your art collection. You know all the artists. Who is good?

2. Well, what sort of stuff do you like?

1. I don't know. I don't know anything about what makes a good artist, a good painting.

2. A good painting is a painting you enjoy looking at.

1. Well, I don't know what I enjoy.

2. Then you're not ready to buy.

1. I wanted to buy a painting with the money I win from this tournament.

2. Whoa. Take it easy. You're not over the finish line yet.

1. I will be.

2. Look. Forget about dealers. Take some time, go to the museums, go to the galleries — whenever you're in a new city take an afternoon — buy yourself a little notebook, write down the names of what you like. Buy some books, educate yourself a little bit. Then we can start talking dealers. Okay?

1. Okay. *(Beat.)* I just like the idea ... I respect that you have this hobby. That you have knowledge of an area outside the game, that you —

2. *(Suddenly angry.)* You don't need a fucking *hobby* right now, all right? Jesus Christ, you ignorant little hayseed! You need to *win.* *(Beat.)*

1. Yes. You're right. *(Beat. He finishes dressing.)* I'm sorry you were eliminated.

2. Guy slapped me around like a bitch. Ran my legs right off. I had to call for a trainer in the fourth set just to catch my breath. I'm lucky there *was* a fourth set. The first two were like those nightmares where you can't wake up. At least they were over fast. You'll face the fucker in the final, probably.

1. He is good, I agree. He is going all the way this time. I will play him there. *(Beat.)* If your nephew would like a ticket, please tell him I will be happy to —

2. Yeah, okay. Thanks. *(Beat.)*

1. Any advice?

2. For you?

1. As you say. I'm not over the finishing line yet. *(Beat.)*

2. I don't think you have anything to worry about. *(Blackout.)*

THREE

1 changing. 2 enters.

2. Well! What do you know.
1. Yes. What do you know.
2. The "old dog" …
1. Yes.
2. Thanks for what you said out there.
1. Of course.
2. You memorize that?
1. No.
2. 'Cause it was eloquent. I mean your English has improved a lot in a short time.
1. Well.
2. And hey, this is the last one. Don't worry.
1. The last one what?
2. I'm announcing I'm retiring at the end of the season.
1. Oh.
2. Tomorrow. We'll do a press conference, whole bit.
1. I see.
2. Feels right. I'd rather go out like this. I'm not operating under any illusions here. I don't think this is, you know, the beginning of the "second act," or —
1. Yes, fine.
2. I mean, yes, I always thought about, you know, "Go around one more time." But it has to be the right way. The last thing you want is to seem desperate or pathetic, crap out in the first round — or worse, the second: pull some kid in the first who's nervous and star-struck and green so you take him down easy, then get my clock cleaned by some coldeyed Russian or Swede, never broke the top ten but a veteran, makes a career getting into the third round of every fucking tournament he enters, he's not about to let me stand in the way of his twenty-four grand, he needs it to pay his coach and his trainer and his nutritionist and his brother who carries his rackets … Listen to me. Babbling away. I guess

143

I'm keyed up. Can you blame me? Anyway, you played a good match.

1. Fuck you. *(Beat.)*

2. Excuse me?

1. You think you won this?

2. Yeah. I do.

1. The call at break point in the fourth —

2. It was in!

1. It was NOT in! The linesman called it out —

2. And he was overruled half a second later, *correctly,* 'cause it was a shitbrained call from the far end of the court, my grandmother was closer to the ball and she's in Phoenix and she's been *dead* for six years.

1. Oh, now you are being ridiculous.

2. *And* the guy's a drunk —

1. I think – "You protest so much."

2. Don't get lippy with me. And it's "protest too much." If you can't handle the loss get off the fucking circuit.

1. No, *you* get off the circuit! You are old man!

2. I *am* getting off. I told you.

1. Good!

2. Yeah — I did you a favor. You forgot what losing feels like. I reminded you.

1. Also your draw was ridiculous.

2. Fuck off.

1. Admit that, at least. It was the joke of the tournament. For last two weeks you could not have gotten a sillier bunch of babies to play. First round — a qualifier, ranked two-oh-five. Second round — American teenager with drug problem.

2. He doesn't have a drug problem.

1. He was arrested in Florida last summer!

2. He's been clean for months!

1. His agent says. I doubt *very* much. But never mind. Round three — your opponent defaulted in the second set, twisted ankle.

2. Because I made him run down that *screaming* backhand volley, shot of the *tournament* —

1. You only play two sets! That is the fact! Fourth round — another old man like you, only not even in shape. Quarters — clay court specialist, shouldn't be here at all. Semis — he is playing injured all

season, and *he* had a *terrible* draw, five sets all the way so he meets you tired. Finals — *me,* your first real opponent.

2. And I won.

1. No, I *lost.* Bad calls. Bad crowd, assholes – they want to see "Grandpapa" win one last time. Bad draw, bad weather, bad everything. All of it. They robbed me.

2. Yeah, I'll tell them that when I cash the check.

1. *(Kicks his equipment bag.)* Fuck *everything.* My coach flies up here to see *this? (Beat. He calms down, retrieves his bag. They dress in silence for a moment..)*

2. How is your coach?

1. He is okay. Holding on. Somehow.

2. Girlfriend?

1. We broke up.

2. Ah. *(Beat.)* You ever buy any paintings?

1. No. Stupid idea. I don't want to be a pretentious art-snob shit, going to stupid galleries, drinking wine. Museums are *fucking* boring. I'm going to buy horses. I want a horse farm in Virginia. This will be *my* "hobby." Fuck paintings and dealers. Fuck *you.* After today, all I can say: I have no respect for you. *(2 looks at him. Beat.)*

2. Attaboy.

End of Play

PROPERTY LIST

Tennis bag
Tennis ball
Sharpie Pen

WEIRD WATER

BY ROBERT LEWIS VAUGHAN

CHARACTERS

HAL — 50s, Tommy's father

LIBBY — 50s, Tommy's mother

JEFF — 25, Tommy's best friend

PLACE

Tommy's bedroom.

WEIRD WATER

Black.

Silence.

Dim light from downstairs comes up and we see a man, Hal, sitting on Tommy's bed. Hal flicks a remote and turns on a television set — the soft glow brightens the room.

We hear a reporter's voice —

MALE REPORTER. Returning to the White House two days early from vacation at his ranch in Crawford, Texas, the President said today the United States would — *(Hal flicks the remote, changes the channel.)*
FEMALE REPORTER. When interviewed from his ranch in Crawford, Texas, about the most recent attacks, the President said — *(Hal flicks the remote again.)*
ANNOUNCER. This is CNN. *(Again.)*
LOCAL NEWS REPORTER. Reporting from Crawford, this is John Jenson for KXIT in Amarillo, the Panhandle's news leader — *(Hal turns off the power to the set. Tommy's room is dark again. A moment. A hallway light comes on. Libby appears in the doorway to the bedroom. She reaches into the room and feels for the light switch. A small bedside lamp comes on. Hal remains sitting on the bed. Libby stands in the doorway. She looks at him. He does not look at her. A moment.)*
HAL. Why the hell do you think he had this small lamp with a dim bulb connected to the light switch instead of the bright desk lamp? Can't see anything. *(She does not leave the doorway.)*
LIBBY. You were sittin' in the dark anyway. What could you see? … How long have you been in here today?
HAL. I think that little lamp could probably stand a bulb with a higher wattage, don't you? What do you think he has in there anyway? twenty-five watts? Think it could stand a sixty?

149

LIBBY. They had Darcy's birthday party at the office today. Sue brought those cookies she made for the Christmas party last year. *(He turns the TV back on and surfs.)* Didn't you say you liked those cookies? I know you said you liked those cookies. She always makes more than she needs to. I brought some home. You remember likin' those cookies? I think I finally talked her into givin' me the dadgum recipe.

HAL. He programmed every news network into this favorite channel button. The History Channel. Didn't he used to call that the "Hitler Channel"? The Discovery Channel. MTV. VH1. And the Golf Channel. I didn't even know there was a Golf Channel. Did you know there was Golf Channel? *(He flicks off the television.)* I didn't know he liked golf so much that he'd set the Golf Channel this way? Did you know he liked golf that much?

LIBBY. … They're the cookies with the — *(He flicks the remote and the television is back on.)*

HAL. Look at this, would you? There's a goddamned Golf Channel. *(The golf commentator's sotto voce ramblings are coming from the TV.)*

LIBBY. How long have you been sitting up here today?

HAL. You home early or somethin'?

LIBBY. It's six-thirty. Didn't you even notice you were sitting in the dark? That the sun went down? Again? *(He switches channels.)* Come on back downstairs with me, Hal. There's somebody —

HAL. Why don't you step foot across the line from the grey carpet in the hallway to the blue carpet in here? Blue. Grey. — In your own son's goddamn room.

LIBBY. Jeff's downstairs.

HAL. How long, Libby?

LIBBY. How long what? … Have you been sittin' in here in the dark?

HAL. Since you came into this room?

LIBBY. You spend enough time in here for both us. *(He changes channels again and she reaches back inside, flips the switch off and walks away leaving him in the dark — except for the glow from the TV screen and the faint light from the hallway. He surfs. A moment.)*

HAL. … Goddamn Golf Channel. *(A moment. A young man walks into the light and stops at the doorway to the bedroom. He's framed in the light from the hall. He's holding a plate of cookies. The young man, Jeff, says nothing, and Hal doesn't notice him. Hal surfs.)*

JEFF. Libby said if I was gonna come on up here to see you I should bring these cookies. *(Jeff steps into the room and turns on the desk lamp. He leans on the desk but does not sit.)*

HAL. What're you doing here, Jeff? I thought you moved to Austin —

JEFF. I came up for the weekend. See Mama and them ...

HAL. Nice of you.

JEFF. Family thing — 'cause ... I got engaged. Lisa — she ... Tommy ... She ...

HAL. I remember Libby saying something about the little gal you were with at ...

JEFF. I guess his funeral was the last time I saw you. Huh?

HAL. You and Tommy went off to school. And you stayed ... in school. You stayed here. You finished up and you're building a life for yourself. Now you're planning to —

JEFF. Next spring.

HAL. Your mama and daddy must be real proud of you.

JEFF. Mama's just goin' crazy and ... *(Pause.)* I'm not gonna have a best man.

HAL. Now why would you go sayin' somethin' like that?

JEFF. He was my best friend since we were what? Six? When we moved in over here across the street? Tommy's my best man, Hal — nobody else is gonna stand where he shouldda been standin'. *(Silence.)* Libby said you been stayin' up here a lot.

HAL. Where he shouldda been standin' ... yes, sir. You might want to write yourself a letter to the drunk driver responsible for that. Yes, sir, you might want to let that man know how you feel about things.

JEFF. Hal ...

HAL. Did you know Tommy had the Golf Channel programmed into this thing, here?

JEFF. I wanted to talk to you more at his funeral. I meant to ... I never ... I didn't know how. I didn't know what to say.

HAL. I don't know what to say either. I still just don't know what to say. You tried them cookies, Jeff?

JEFF. I tried to talk him out of it. I wanted him to stay in school with me.

HAL. Libby tried to talk him out of it, too.

JEFF. He made up his own mind.

HAL. That's what I taught my son to do ... make up his own mind.

JEFF. He loved you so much for that. I wish me and my dad — we —

HAL. Y'all used to butt heads. You two getting along any better?

JEFF. Well. He's always gonna wanna tell me how to do things. He still doesn't listen to what I have to say —

HAL. Runnin' a business — he's runnin' a business, Jeff. Everybody's gotta run a business. Maybe I shoulda —

JEFF. How's the store doin'?

HAL. Jerry's my right hand down there — don't know what I'd do without him. People're always gonna need trophies. Schools — businesses — all the social clubs. And … World's Best Moms … World's Best Dads …

JEFF. My old man's still … I always envied Tommy and you. Did you know that? Did Tommy ever say anything to you about that?

HAL. Not a thing.

JEFF. Well, maybe it was —

HAL. Your daddy tried to teach you everything he knew. Didn't he? He has a strong will and strong beliefs — and he wanted you to …

JEFF. You did that with Tommy —

HAL. Libby and I never — we taught Tommy to think for himself. We didn't think we should … spoon feed him. We wanted him to ask questions.

JEFF. And he did. All the time. About everything.

HAL. I didn't tell him he shouldn't join the army.

JEFF. Why? *(Pause.)* Why didn't you try to talk him out of it, Hal? He'd've listen to you. I know he'd've listened to you.

HAL. And I feel like I helped murder my son.

JEFF. — Hal. I didn't mean —

HAL. It's a game. That's all it is, Jeff — a playground game. Follow the leader. But who in the hell was he followin'?

JEFF. It's because of Pat Tillman. When he heard what Tillman did? That he got killed — it's … that's what it was. That guy gave up millions and walked away from his football career: Tommy thought that was unbelievable — it was all over the news. The interviews. Why he gave it up to join and … by the time people found out about what really happened to Tillman — it was too late. Wasn't it? For Tommy.

HAL. He knew I had serious doubts about what the hell we were doing over there. He didn't ask me any questions about that though. I didn't try to explain myself to him. Diving in like that — I should have put my foot down. You're supposed to trust your leader. I'm a business man. I own a trophy shop. We have a good home and a good life and I thought I was raisin' my son to have the … even-handed … views I have — had. I thought I was a good leader — good husband

and dad. Think for yourself, son — think about things — if you think about things, you'll know what's right. You'll do what's right. How can this be right now? This ain't right, Jeff. This ain't at all right.

JEFF. Yes, sir.

HAL. Pat Tillman was his hero.

JEFF. Yes — after he heard what he gave up. And then he died. But he wasn't even in the war — was he? He was in Afghanistan. Tommy was in the war.

HAL. I'm not sure what war this is. *(Pause.)* You heard me and your daddy go at a few times over the years.

JEFF. You sure can frustrate my old man, Hal. I love that. *(Hal gets up and opens the bottom drawer of his son's dresser. He pulls out a bottle of whiskey. He opens it and drinks then gives the bottle to Jeff, who takes a small swig.)* Between you and me, I'm surprised we never gave him a stroke.

HAL. Your daddy came to see me a couple of days after the funeral service … His opinions and his commitment were deeper than I'd ever seen 'em. We sat downstairs in the den and sipped scotch. I listened to him. Talking about how proud he was of Tommy. And I listened to him. I looked at your daddy, Jeff, and I had no clue about who in hell he was. *(Pause.)* A man I'd known for fifteen or sixteen some-odd years. Tellin' me how proud he was of my son. I never said much. Let your daddy do all the talking. Couple days after Tommy's funeral. I think I was still numb. Maybe I thought he could explain to me why I was wrong in thinkin' what I'd been thinkin'. Maybe If I listened to him I'd understand …

JEFF. Sure enough?

HAL. When he left he tried his best to give me a hug. He couldn't bring himself to do it — shoved his hand out so we could shake. Told me again how proud he was of us and of Tommy — for what he'd done for our country.

JEFF. He shakes my hand too …

HAL. I closed the door and walked upstairs. Came in here and sat on the bed. Numb. That was the night I knew I'd lost more than my son. My boy. Somethin' — gone …

JEFF. Maybe I should —

HAL. You're not goin' anywhere, Jeff. *(Hal hands the bottle back to Jeff. Jeff takes the bottle and sips. He sits in the chair at the desk.)* Follow the leader, remember? Schoolyard games to teach you discipline and character — leadership. Just because I didn't vote for the man, doesn't mean — didn't mean that I … I tried to relax myself into the fact that he was presidin' over us for his terms in office, and he's a goddamned liar, Jeff. Pretendin' to be a real Texan and he's from goddamn Connecticut? That shouldda been everybody's first clue right there — he's just nothin' but a pretender — pretendin' he knows what the hell he's doin'. And I didn't stop my son from … I let him go — I let him make his own decision and —

JEFF. Maybe Libby could — maybe you should talk to —

HAL. Libby can't have this conversation with me. Libby doesn't know who I am anymore. Do you know who I am?

JEFF. You're my best man's dad. You're my friend, too. The guy I thought sometimes, when I was a kid, that I could talk to about things when I couldn't talk to my own dad? You helped me a lot, Hal.

HAL. That's who I used to be, Jeff. The night your daddy stopped by for a visit — I shook his hand and said good night and realized I had nothing left — I don't know anything. I don't even believe in anything anymore.

JEFF. Yes, you do, Hal — I know you …

HAL. I spend time in this room looking … I keep thinking I'll find it again — understand. I know you loved him.

JEFF. He was my brother — if I was going to have a brother — he was my brother.

HAL. I stared at you all during his funeral. Your little gal holding your hand in both of hers. She was so lost. Libby's hand was so cold in mine. Your little gal … she didn't know what to do with you — being such a mess. Had she ever seen you cry?

JEFF. I sure was a mess, wasn't I? No — she … no. I didn't know I could cry … like that.

HAL. Now see? If I knew who I was — I'd know what happened. I don't know what I'm gonna find in this room. But I'm waitin' to believe again. Even though I don't know what I'm gonna find. Is Tommy's ghost gonna come see me sittin' in here and kick my ass back into my life? Say "Daddy, what the hell're you doin'? Go make a trophy. Some kid just won a spellin' bee — some kid needs you." I can't do it. Jeff, I can't do it.

JEFF. Hal, I —

HAL. It's a brain tumor.

JEFF. I'm sorry…?

HAL. It's a car wreck.

JEFF. Hal?

HAL. If Tommy got a brain tumor and died of cancer — I'd know how — I'd know why. If he got in a car wreck ... I'd feel cheated and robbed, but I'd understand. If I'd been born in the 1920s and lost my son in World War Two — I'd know — I'd understand — I think. But now. Not now. Because it just don't make a lick of sense to me, and that makes me ... I'm treadin' water, boy — new, weird water, and I'm sick and tired and I feel like I'm just about to drown. I can see the shore in the distance, but it's too far away. Libby's waving her arms trying to get my attention, but I can't hear her calling me — because I'm too far out in the water.

JEFF. She needs you, Hal. Libby —

HAL. That's your little gal in the picture on the bulletin board?

JEFF. Yeah. I ... *(Jeff loses it a little and takes the bottle.)* I feel so fucked up about this right now ... I ... somebody took my ... from six years old ... I don't know what you feel inside, Hal, but I ... A brain cancer — or a car wreck ... I get it. I could — yeah. Yeah ...

HAL. It is a car wreck — with a drunk driver — Bush is behind that wheel and he drove right into Iraq. You ever notice how when a drunk causes a wreck — most of the time they come off without a scratch or maybe a little beat up, but — it's everybody else who suffers or dies? But just about everybody seemed fine tellin' him he was okay to drive, didn't they? *(Silence. Jeff takes a photo off the bulletin board.)*

JEFF. One of the summers Tommy and I worked for you at your store.

HAL. You're ...

JEFF. I 'member this T-shirt. I think this was the summer you — it is — we were takin' the recyclin' out to the alley and you caught us tryin' to smoke weed for the first time.

HAL. Let me see that. *(They trade the bottle for the photo.)* I'll be goddamned.

JEFF. You never told my dad about that.

HAL. Hell no. *(Pause.)* Maybe you should think about askin' your daddy to be your best man.

JEFF. I made my decision. ... I want you and Libby to come to the wedding, you know. Lisa really, really loved Tommy, too, and ...

HAL. I wouldn't miss it for the world.

JEFF. I should ...

HAL. Did he ever say anything to you about ... anything? Did I ever — I feel so ... I just flat out feel cheated. ... Years and years and years. And I ...

JEFF. ... I ... *(Jeff shakes his head.)* I should ... Mama's makin' supper. I just wanted to come by and see you. Say hi and let you know that ... I was gonna honor Tommy this way. Let you know that his place beside me was ... still his. Oh, and Mama wanted me to ask you and Libby if you wanted to come over — join us for supper. She said it'd been too long.

HAL. Did you ask Libby? What'd Libby say?

JEFF. She told me to ask you.

HAL. You tell your mama and daddy we said thank you but we got ... thank her for us ...?

JEFF. I will. Um. I was thinking about going out to ... to see Tommy's ... grave ... on Sunday before I ... would you come on out there with me, maybe? *(Silence.)*

Okay. Well ... I should ...

HAL. I might want to take a drive on out there with you.

JEFF. That'd be ... appreciate that.

HAL. Before you go: This goddamn thing here ... *(He picks up another remote.)* I can't for the life of me get this thing to work. I know what he watched. I was wondering ... last time he was home — what he was listenin' to. I know there's one of them CD disks in there ... *(Jeff sits on the bed next to Hal.)*

JEFF. See this button. Press it ... then press this one — whatever was playing ... last time he was home ... *(Jeff hugs Hal and heads for the door. He stops.)* So, I'll stop on by Sunday mornin' then? *(Hal nods. Jeff walks out. A moment. Hal flicks the button on the remote to Tommy's sound system. He presses play. A song like Jamie Cullum's "All At Sea" begins to play.* Hal gets up and tacks the photo back on the bulletin board. He listens to the song, looking away from the photos. He opens the desk drawer and pokes around a moment. He stops and looks at something, then pulls out a bottle of cologne. He looks at the label as he closes the desk drawer. Hal contemplates the bottle of cologne. He looks at the CD player and stops the song with the remote. He sits on the bed and looks around Tommy's room. Silence. Hal pulls the cap from the bottle of cologne and breathes it in. He sprays his son's fragrance into the air and breathes it in again. The lights fade away.)*

End of Play

---

* See Special Note on Songs and Recordings on copyright page.

PROPERTY LIST

TV remotes
Plate of cookies
Whiskey bottle
Photo
Bottle of cologne

SOUND EFFECTS

TV announcers' voices, male and female
TV reporters' voices, male and female
Golf commentator

APPENDIX

AMATEURS and AN UPSET Copyright © 2012, David Auburn. Inquiries concerning all other rights for AMATEURS and AN UPSET should be addressed to Paradigm, 360 Park Avenue South, 16th Floor, New York, NY 10010. Attn: Jonathan Mills.

BOLERO and THE GREEN HILL Copyright © 2001, David Ives. Inquiries concerning all other rights for BOLERO and THE GREEN HILL should be addressed to Abrams Artists Agency, 275 Seventh Avenue, 26th Floor, New York, NY 10001. Attn: Sarah L. Douglas.

BREAKFAST AND BED Copyright © 2012, Amy Fox. Inquiries concerning all other rights for BREAKFAST AND BED should be addressed to the Author c/o Dramatists Play Service, Inc., 440 Park Avenue South, New York, NY 10016.

CELL Copyright © 2012, Cassandra Medley. Inquiries concerning all other rights for CELL should be addressed to the Author c/o Dramatists Play Service, Inc., 440 Park Avenue South, New York, NY 10016.

DIVERSIONS Copyright © 1995, Christopher Durang. Christopher Durang's author's note for DIVERSIONS was originally published by Smith and Kraus, Inc. in *Twenty-Seven Short Plays*. Inquiries concerning all other rights for DIVERSIONS should be addressed to Helen Merrill LLC c/o ICM Partners, 730 Fifth Avenue, New York, NY 10019. Attn: Patrick Herold.

A SECOND OF PLEASURE Copyright © 2012, Neil LaBute. Inquiries concerning all other rights for A SECOND OF PLEASURE should be addressed to The Gersh Agency, 41 Madison Avenue, 33rd Floor, New York, NY 10010. Attn: Joyce Ketay.

WEIRD WATER Copyright © 2012, Robert Lewis Vaughan. Inquiries concerning all other rights for WEIRD WATER should be addressed to The Gersh Agency, 41 Madison Avenue, 33rd Floor, New York, NY 10010. Attn: Joyce Ketay.

HAPPY Copyright © 2012, Alan Zweibel. Inquiries concerning all other rights for HAPPY should be addressed to Paradigm, 360 Park Avenue South, 16th Floor, New York, NY 10010. Attn: Jonathan Mills.

NEW PLAYS

★ **I'LL EAT YOU LAST: A CHAT WITH SUE MENGERS by John Logan.** For more than 20 years, Sue Mengers' clients were the biggest names in show business: Barbra Streisand, Faye Dunaway, Burt Reynolds, Ali MacGraw, Gene Hackman, Cher, Candice Bergen, Ryan O'Neal, Nick Nolte, Mike Nichols, Gore Vidal, Bob Fosse…If her clients were the talk of the town, she was the town, and her dinner parties were the envy of Hollywood. Now, you're invited into her glamorous Beverly Hills home for an evening of dish, dirty secrets and all the inside showbiz details only Sue can tell you. "A delectable soufflé of a solo show…thanks to the buoyant, witty writing of Mr. Logan" –NY Times. "80 irresistible minutes of primo tinseltown dish from a certified master chef." –Hollywood Reporter. [1W] ISBN: 978-0-8222-3079-3

★ **PUNK ROCK by Simon Stephens.** In a private school outside of Manchester, England, a group of highly-articulate seventeen-year-olds flirt and posture their way through the day while preparing for their A-Level mock exams. With hormones raging and minimal adult supervision, the students must prepare for their future — and survive the savagery of high school. Inspired by playwright Simon Stephens' own experiences as a teacher, PUNK ROCK is an honest and unnerving chronicle of contemporary adolescence. "[A] tender, ferocious and frightning play." –NY Times. "[A] muscular little play that starts out funny and ferocious then reveals its compassion by degrees." –Hollywood Reporter. [5M, 3W] ISBN: 978-0-8222-3288-9

★ **THE COUNTRY HOUSE by Donald Margulies.** A brood of famous and longing-to-be-famous creative artists have gathered at their summer home during the Williamstown Theatre Festival. When the weekend takes an unexpected turn, everyone is forced to improvise, inciting a series of simmering jealousies, romantic outbursts, and passionate soul-searching. Both witty and compelling, THE COUNTRY HOUSE provides a piercing look at a family of performers coming to terms with the roles they play in each other's lives. "A valentine to the artists of the stage." –NY Times. "Remarkably candid and funny." –Variety. [3M, 3W] ISBN: 978-0-8222-3274-2

★ **OUR LADY OF KIBEHO by Katori Hall.** Based on real events, OUR LADY OF KIBEHO is an exploration of faith, doubt, and the power and consequences of both. In 1981, a village girl in Rwanda claims to see the Virgin Mary. Ostracized by her schoolmates and labeled disturbed, everyone refuses to believe, until impossible happenings appear again and again. Skepticism gives way to fear, and then to belief, causing upheaval in the school community and beyond. "Transfixing." –NY Times. "Hall's passionate play renews belief in what theater can do." –Time Out [7M, 8W, 1 boy] ISBN: 978-0-8222-3301-5

DRAMATISTS PLAY SERVICE, INC.
440 Park Avenue South, New York, NY 10016 212-683-8960 Fax 212-213-1539
postmaster@dramatists.com www.dramatists.com

NEW PLAYS

★ **AGES OF THE MOON by Sam Shepard.** Byron and Ames are old friends, reunited by mutual desperation. Over bourbon on ice, they sit, reflect and bicker until fifty years of love, friendship and rivalry are put to the test at the barrel of a gun. "A poignant and honest continuation of themes that have always been present in the work of one of this country's most important dramatists, here reconsidered in the light and shadow of time passed." –NY Times. "Finely wrought…as enjoyable and enlightening as a night spent stargazing." –Talkin' Broadway. [2M] ISBN: 978-0-8222-2462-4

★ **ALL THE WAY by Robert Schenkkan. Winner of the 2014 Tony Award for Best Play.** November, 1963. An assassin's bullet catapults Lyndon Baines Johnson into the presidency. A Shakespearean figure of towering ambition and appetite, this charismatic, conflicted Texan hurls himself into the passage of the Civil Rights Act—a tinderbox issue emblematic of a divided America—even as he campaigns for re-election in his own right, and the recognition he so desperately wants. In Pulitzer Prize and Tony Award–winning Robert Schenkkan's vivid dramatization of LBJ's first year in office, means versus ends plays out on the precipice of modern America. ALL THE WAY is a searing, enthralling exploration of the morality of power. It's not personal, it's just politics. "…action-packed, thoroughly gripping… jaw-dropping political drama." –Variety. "A theatrical coup…nonstop action. The suspense of a first-class thriller." –NY1. [17M, 3W] ISBN: 978-0-8222-3181-3

★ **CHOIR BOY by Tarell Alvin McCraney.** The Charles R. Drew Prep School for Boys is dedicated to the creation of strong, ethical black men. Pharus wants nothing more than to take his rightful place as leader of the school's legendary gospel choir. Can he find his way inside the hallowed halls of this institution if he sings in his own key? "[An] affecting and honest portrait…of a gay youth tentatively beginning to find the courage to let the truth about himself become known." –NY Times. "In his stirring and stylishly told drama, Tarell Alvin McCraney cannily explores race and sexuality and the graces and gravity of history." –NY Daily News. [7M] ISBN: 978-0-8222-3116-5

★ **THE ELECTRIC BABY by Stefanie Zadravec.** When Helen causes a car accident that kills a young man, a group of fractured souls cross paths and connect around a mysterious dying baby who glows like the moon. Folk tales and folklore weave throughout this magical story of sad endings, strange beginnings and the unlikely people that get you from one place to the next. "The imperceptible magic that pervades human existence and the power of myth to assuage sorrow are invoked by the playwright as she entwines the lives of strangers in THE ELECTRIC BABY, a touching drama." –NY Times. "As dazzling as the dialogue is dreamful." –Pittsburgh City Paper. [3M, 3W] ISBN: 978-0-8222-3011-3

DRAMATISTS PLAY SERVICE, INC.
440 Park Avenue South, New York, NY 10016 212-683-8960 Fax 212-213-1539
postmaster@dramatists.com www.dramatists.com